PLAYING IN THE APOCALYPSE

KATE COMINGS

DEDICATION

For all the people of Isla Vista, past and present.

CONTENTS

AUTHOR'S NOTE

This book is about my senior year at UCSB. It was 1970, the year of the riots. The events in the book happened to my friends and me and are as accurate as my memory will allow, but I have changed the names and some identifying details of most of the people, and some of the characters are composites.

1

SAN FRANCISCO, 1969

Joel and I were lovers during the riots when I was a student at UC Santa Barbara. The riots happened in Isla Vista, a densely packed, beachfront ghetto of cheaply built student housing next to the university campus. My apartment was right on the police riot patrol loop. Armored trucks circled the neighborhood again and again. During those nights, they would lob tear gas canisters into people's yards and onto porches and balconies. The gas leaked in around the doors and windows of the crummy apartments, and we lay on the floor holding wet towels over our faces in order to breathe. Outside, the police shot the tires of parked cars and gunned down dogs or cats that wandered out on the streets. Our town was under siege. No one was safe. Nothing was safe.

In Southeast Asia, the Vietnam War raged on and on. Joel and I first met at the San Francisco marina on a chilly November morning in 1969. We had both come from Santa Barbara—miles north—for the Vietnam War Moratorium. He rode up with a buddy; I arrived in a van full of strangers.

On Highway 101 north of Santa Barbara, I ride in the van's back seat next to a guy named Bill. He has just started to grow a beard; maybe two days' worth of stubble blackens his cheeks and chin. A gold watch peeks out from under his green flannel shirt cuff. I don't know Bill or any of the other people in the van.

Outside San Luis Obispo is the enormous pink-and-white Madonna Inn with its gables, diamond-shaped glass panes, and towers. It looks like somebody snatched it out of Disneyland during the night and dropped it here in the middle of the barren landscape. My mother loves to come here.

"Headquarters of the silent majority," I say. No one answers. The guys in the van don't even glance at the Madonna Inn.

I sink back into my seat and sigh.

I do a lot of things on impulse, and this morning, I bummed a last-minute ride from the University of California at Santa Barbara to the Moratorium march in San Francisco with a bunch of guys I've never seen before in my life. It was a sudden, hasty decision to be one of the thousands, maybe millions, protesting the war. After Nixon's asinine bragging about the "silent majority" who support his policies, I couldn't miss the chance to put myself out there and take a stand. I went to the meet-up spot for drivers and passengers, a vacant lot behind the health food store in Isla Vista, the student community next to the campus. I walked up to a safe-looking, bearded guy with sandy hair and a sad look on his face.

"Hi, I'm Kate." I rubbed my toe in the dust.

"Chris," he said.

"Can you give me a ride to San Francisco?"

"Maybe." There was no interest in his eyes when he looked at me; I could have been an old piece of wood lying in the dirt. "Have you got any gas money?"

"I can give you ten dollars," I said.

"Okay. Van's right over there, get in. Gotta warn you, though, this won't be a social trip. A friend of ours just got killed over in Vietnam."

"Oh, how awful!" I reached out to touch his arm but he stepped back.

"Yeah," was all he said before he walked away.

On the ride north, Bill, Chris, and Larry all talk about their dead friend Jeremy, their buddy since high school. They've forgotten all about me. The air in the van burns with sorrow and feels heavy and sad when I breathe it in, giving me a whole new reason to march. Of all the rides I could have picked, I ended up with these guys.

The van pulls into the city late at night and parks at the marina. Four of us squeeze into the rear space to try and get some sleep. I'm jammed between two guys I don't know with no room even to roll over. In the suffocating darkness, I can almost feel the metal sides of the van pressing in like the inside of a coffin. Tight spaces terrify me. I grab my pack and sleeping bag, slide open the door, and crawl over Bill out onto the cold, dark pavement. I suck in long, deep gasps of salty, cold air. As I ease the door closed, the guys relax into the added space. "Much better," one of them mumbles.

My relief on getting out of the van lasts only seconds before I realize it's the middle of the night and I'm all alone. *Now* what am I going to do? The parking lot is full of cars. Have they all come for the moratorium? Or could someone be lurking behind one of those dark windshields? I stride across the pavement toward the marina. Lights on the boats make sparkly reflections in the black water. I spread out my sleeping bag on a grassy spot and crawl inside. It's cold, and I shiver, then go rigid when a car door clicks shut somewhere behind me. Leather soles creak on pavement. My stomach clenches into a hard ball and my heart tries to batter its way out of my chest. But the footsteps head away and fade into the distance. Safe for now—but this is almost worse than suffocating in that van. What in the world was I thinking, coming here all by myself? I don't even have a clue where to find the march! And how am I ever going to get back home?

I burrow into the bag, hiding my face and hair so no one will be able to tell whether I'm male or female, and squirm until I find a spot on the lumpy ground where nothing jabs into me. This was supposed to be a big adventure. Coming up here on a whim felt like the ultimate freedom—but now I'd give anything to be back in my safe apartment, in my own bed!

Waves lap and splash against the hulls of the anchored boats. Chains creak and moan. Old Italian songs drift across the water; a man's tenor throbs with passion and tender sadness. I picture a cozy scene with burly fishermen clustered around a table with bottles of beer, their catch all in, songs of home playing on the radio… The music comforts me.

It's a long time before I drift off to sleep. When I wake up, it's still night. It's dark and cold and the music has stopped. I burrow deeper into the bag, wrap my arms around myself and shiver. It feels like forever before the sky gets lighter. A gray mist hangs over the water.

I sit on my rumpled orange sleeping bag near the edge of the marina, tugging on my boots. Cold mist drifts in from the ocean; the grass is wet and the outside of my sleeping bag is damp and slick. I gaze out across the gray-green, choppy water. Far to my left, the red pillars of the Golden Gate Bridge peek through the fog.

I'm groggy and disoriented after my night on the hard ground. My eyes feel full of sand from not enough sleep and I blink to get rid of the gritty feeling. I take deep breaths of moist, salty air. As the heavy mist begins to lift, gasoline engines rumble into life, and one by one, the fishing boats head out across the water.

A car door slams behind me. "Oh fuck," somebody mumbles under his breath. I look over my shoulder. It's a guy in a blue Levi's jacket. He paws through a brown canvas satchel. "Fuck fuck fuck." He sets the bag down, looks up, and catches me staring.

"Hi," he says.

What a fox! Long, tangled, slept-on blond hair hangs in his face; his nose is like a hawk's beak.

"Uh, Hi," I say. "What's up?"

"Do you have a hairbrush? I forgot to pack one." He gives me a rueful little smile that has me smiling back right away.

"I hope so." I find the brush in my daypack and hand it to him. He grips the wooden handle and drags the bristles through his hair. Rumpled hair doesn't hurt his looks a bit. I use my hands to smooth my own long, brown hair as I gaze out over the water. The boats head toward the bridge and the open sea beyond. The haunting Italian music still plays in my head. It was the last thing I heard before I fell asleep.

"Thanks a lot!" The blond guy's voice interrupts my daze. "I don't know how I managed to make it up here without a hairbrush." He's brushed his hair back, away from his tanned, high-cheekboned face. He hands me the brush.

"No problem," I say. "I forget stuff all the time." I use the brush to tease the knots out of my own tangled rats nest. Strands of our hair, blond and dark brown, twine among the bristles. "You here for the moratorium?"

"Yeah, that's our van over there." He gestures toward a yellow VW bus with a hand-lettered sign taped in the window, "Pull Out Dick."

I start to laugh. "Good sign!"

"You like it? I made that one up myself. I'm Joel, by the way."

"I'm Kate." I kneel on the ground and roll up my sleeping bag. "I really need some coffee. Hope there's an open café near here."

"Coffee sounds good. Want some company?"

"I'd love company."

Joel stows his satchel and my sleeping bag in the van. "Dude I came with is still out cold," he says. "Bet the march'll be over by the time he wakes up."

I shiver in my unlined, fringed suede jacket as we walk through the parking lot and up a street past locked-up shops with bars on the doors. It is still early morning. Puffs of steam rise every time we exhale. I bite down hard to stop my teeth from chattering. "I hitched a ride up here from UC Santa Barbara," I say. "I didn't think about how much colder it would be."

"Really? I'm from there, too!" He stops and stares at me. "What a trip—I mean, what are the chances of that happening?"

Wow. If only I could have ridden up with him instead! "Yeah," I say. "It's pretty amazing. This is turning out to be an incredible adventure."

"That's how I feel, too. I've never even been to San Francisco before."

"I've been a couple of times as a kid with my parents, which is the same as never being here."

We walk until we come to the Doggie Diner, a dingy little restaurant with a huge wiener-dog head mounted on the roof. The Doggie Diner is open.

In a minute, we're seated at a tiny green Formica table, sipping strong, bitter coffee that tastes like it has been sitting on the burner all night. It's hot though, that's the main thing, and the white paper cups warm our cold hands. The only other customers are two middle-aged men in baseball caps.

"So…" Joel gives me a considering look. "You hitchhiked up here and just bedded down where they dropped you off? That's a crazy thing to do."

"Not exactly. I could've slept in the back of the van with everybody else, but it was a really tight squeeze and I got claustrophobia. That's why I ended up outside…" I shrug. "Still crazy, I know. I was scared shitless."

"So here we are in a totally foreign city, at least to us," he says. "We might as well be somewhere in Europe."

"Like Italy? The fishing boats had 'O Sole Mio' playing last night."

"I heard that music; it was really cool. So, Italy… or maybe fucking Sweden—it's so cold." Intense blue eyes hold mine. "Let's make this an adventure. Wander around and look at stuff. The march doesn't start for a couple of hours."

I finish the last of my coffee and set the cup down on the worn Formica tabletop. It has left a sour taste in my mouth but I feel a lot warmer. "I could really dig that!" I say.

Joel searches through his pockets. With a look of chagrin, he puts both hands on the table and sighs. "This *is* embarrassing. All I've got is some change—I forgot to bring my wallet. I don't know what we'll eat. Hairbrush, money... I wonder what else I forgot? I feel like a real loser."

"I've got a couple of dollars," I say. "We can pool that with what you have; we'll manage."

Providence must be smiling on our adventure because a few blocks away, I spot a ten-dollar bill on the sidewalk right outside an Italian grocery. The aroma of cured meats and hard, aged cheese draws us in. The dim, shrine-like interior with squeaky dark wood floors is full of treasures—pastas in all shapes and sizes, pickles floating in brine, and bottles of wine. Enormous salamis dangle from hooks on the ceiling. We buy mozzarella cheese and a round loaf of panettone, an airy, sweet bread studded with candied fruit.

The fog has cleared. Joel and I wander until we discover the Russian Hill neighborhood. We meander up and down steep, narrow lanes and stairways beneath tall trees, looking at rich people's homes while we rip off big chunks of panettone to savor with chewy bites of cheese.

"So," Joel says, "do you live in Isla Vista?"

"Yeah," I say. "I'm in one of those duplexes on Sabado Tarde."

"Wow—I live on Del Playa, just a block down." He grins. "We're just a couple of blocks away from each other. I can't believe I never met you before!"

"Yeah, isn't that weird?" I pull a strip of mozzarella off the ball of cheese and stuff it into my mouth. "It took going to San Francisco for us to run into each other! So... what's your major?"

"Philosophy—" He holds up his hand before I can say anything. "Yeah, I know, it's a dead end. I did it to piss off my parents."

"I'm doing English lit," I say. "Not much you can do with that either. How come you want to stick it to your parents?"

"They don't exactly groove on my situation. As far as I was concerned, high school was a colossal waste of time—all this irrelevant crap that you're never going to use… the folks kept saying 'you're never going to amount to anything. With those miserable grades you'll end up washing dishes in a restaurant IF you're lucky.' Fuck them. But then I found out I need to go to college to keep from being drafted. So I signed up to take the SAT—you don't need to have top grades if you ace the SAT. Dad just laughed at me. He said, 'Dream on! You'll never pass. In fact, if you get a high SAT score I'll even buy you a car—that's how sure I am you're in for a rude awakening.'" Joel rips off a chunk of cheese and chomps down on it like he wants to hurt somebody. "I'm a really good test taker," he says, his mouth full. He scowls, and his lips go up, down and sideways as he chews. "I aced that motherfucker, got accepted at UCSB, and my dad had to get me a VW Bug."

I suck in my breath. "I totally relate. My folks kept drumming it into me that without that degree, I'd spend my whole life as a motel maid. I went to Santa Barbara to get away from them."

"Looks like we've got a lot in common."

Back at the marina, I stand outside while Joel gets into the bus to wake up his friend Greg. He comes out by himself. "Greg says for us to go without him. Says he's not into marching all that way. He'll find us later, at the rally."

We follow people meandering along the streets, never sure we're going the right way until we find the huge throng marching down Van Ness Avenue. The march stretches as far as we can see, both ahead and behind, an endless sea of signs and faces. Peace symbols are everywhere along with "Veterans for Peace," "Another Mother for Peace," and "End the War Now." All ages of people jam the street, from toddlers on their dads' shoulders to old people. Along with the huge number of long-haired freaks like us, there are straight business people. Thousands and thousands of people have come to protest the war. I never expected to see professional-looking people marching, men and women in business suits—and people old enough to be my parents. Seeing those older people here brings tears to my eyes. I didn't know that any of them cared—but here are "cool" people from my parents' generation. If only my parents were like them! The police keeping order are friendly too. They smile and flash the peace sign.

Joel takes my hand. "Let's not get separated," he says. "We'd never find each other again."

I squeeze his hand; he squeezes back. "Don't let go," I say.

We thread our way into the crowd, Joel in front, clearing the way. Someone shouts "No war!" and we all march in time, chanting "No war! No War! No war!" Some of the people wear black armbands to honor soldiers who have died.

The march goes on for miles. Along the way, communists pass out pamphlets. I take one and stuff it in my jacket pocket. A very tall, bearded man in a blue headband with light brown hair that hangs past his shoulders hands Joel a joint. "Peace!" he says, and then he's gone, lost in the crowd.

Joel leans in close, his mouth almost touching my ear. "Want to stop for a minute and have a toke?"

I grin. "Of course."

We make our way sideways through the crowd until we see a side street. We leave the march and duck into a doorway. I fish around in my pocket for the book of matches I picked up at the Italian grocery this morning. I hand it to Joel. He puts the joint in his mouth and strikes a match. The orange flame flares up, but the joint won't light, even with five or six tries. "Fucking joint is damp," Joel says.

"Bummer," I say. "We better leave it—we don't want to be carrying, just in case anything happens."

"You're right." He lays the joint down on the doorsill. "That's cool. It'll dry out here and be a nice surprise for whoever finds it."

We hold hands as we walk back to the march. Several men carry a green banner that is spread across the width of the street— "Homosexuals Against the War." A man in a green dress and white pumps prances behind the banner. He's not wearing any underwear. We wait for them to pass, then squeeze back into the crowd where people make room for us.

The march ends with a big rally in the Golden Gate Park polo field. Never have I seen so many people in one place, all gathered together for one cause. An ocean of people stretches to the horizon, as far as I can see in every direction. Joel and I are a long way from the stage. It's hard to hear the rally speakers, so we just sit cross-legged on the short, just-mowed grass. It's still a little damp from the fog this morning, but we didn't bring a blanket. Some of the demonstrators have brought Thermoses and sandwiches wrapped in wax paper. The cast of the rock musical, "Hair" files onto the stage and a woman with a huge Afro belts out the opening bars of "Aquarius."[1] They all dance, arms lifted high, and weave in and out in a mesmerizing pattern.

I lean back on my hands and stretch my legs out in front of me. A helicopter crosses the blue sky far above us. I lean my weight on my left arm, raise my right hand, and flash the Peace sign. All over the park, people wave, two fingers extended in a "V". The chopper gets smaller as it speeds off into the distance. I'm glad now that I grabbed the first ride I could find instead of staying safe in Santa Barbara. It was worth the scary, lonely night on the marina to be here in the middle of this huge multitude all gathered to stop the war. What we're doing is so important. Maybe we're making history today, and I'm sharing this incredible moment with Joel. His eyes are glued to the stage. The dancers are all beautiful, dressed in gorgeous hippie clothes, and every one of them can sing—oh, can they ever sing! I don't know what will happen after Joel and I go back to our university lives, but he's here with me today. I'll never forget him, even if I never see him again.

The cast of Hair leaves the stage and Phil Ochs comes on with his guitar and swings into "I Ain't Marching Anymore."[2] Joel stretches his legs out. His leg bumps mine and stays there. Neither of us moves away. I lean back and slide my arms down so I'm resting on my elbows and forearms. I look up at Joel and smile.

He smiles back. "Jesus—isn't this incredible?"

"I'm in awe—" I say. "There must be a million people here! Nixon *has* to end the war after this."

"I hope so," he says. "I really, really hope so." He leans in toward me, holding my gaze until our lips meet. As we kiss, I turn toward him, lift my left hand and touch his shoulder and his tangled hair. He tastes sweet, like panettone. "I sure didn't expect to find someone like you in San Francisco," he whispers, lips tickling my ear.

"Glad you did, though," I whisper back. I push myself up, bend my knees, roll onto them and face him. He turns toward me too and we rise up on our knees. I wrap my arms around his back and he holds my waist and we kiss again in that crowded spot, surrounded by people on every side. Joy wells up inside me; I feel I'm about to burst. Being together for something so crucial, to end the war, takes our embrace to a different level. This is bigger than just us. Our holding each other here in the middle of this huge gathering could send out a signal for people to care for each other and in some small way, help end the war.

We sit back down as another helicopter flies overhead. We both wave and flash the peace sign. "Do we have any of that bread left?" Joel asks.

I dig into my daypack and take out what's left of the panettone and the ball of mozzarella cheese.

The soft bread with its sweet chunks of fruit tastes wonderful. I let the bread melt in my mouth and then savor the pieces of candied fruit one by one. Joel passes me a hunk of cheese. "You better have some of this before I eat it all." I pull off a piece and put it in my mouth. Sweet and salty, squishy and chewy... the bread and cheese go together so well. I lean my head on Joel's shoulder.

When the rally is over, we make our way out through the crowd. "I don't see how we'll ever find Greg," Joel says. "We may have to hitchhike back."

We come to a path. "Let's wait here," I say. "Maybe we'll see Greg or somebody else we know going by."

We stand next to the path where an endless sea of faces streams past us on their way out of the park. The river of people puts me into a trance. I feel stoned, hypnotized, and still they come. I don't see a single person I know. I'm sure we'll end up hitchhiking, but I'm not worried. Lots of people will be heading south; getting a ride should be easy.

"There he is!" Joel waves; swings his hand back and forth in a wide arc. "Greg!" he shouts. "Greg! Hey—over here!"

Greg turns out to be a tall, tanned surfer. He walks up to us and does a double take when he sees me.

"Hey, Greg—thought we'd never find you," Joel says. "This is Kate; Kate—this is Greg."

"Hi," I say.

Greg's eyes move up and down as he looks me over. "Whoa, I might have known," he jokes. "Leave it to you to score a chick."

Joel gives his arm a punch. "You snooze, you lose! But shit, Greg. Kate and I only just met."

Now we're ready to leave. The path is narrow, and everyone is crowded together in a jostling mass like cattle in a chute as more and more people join the hundreds heading out of the park. Joel and I hold hands and we follow Greg, who's a couple of steps ahead of us as we make our slow way up the path. At last we come to a road. The people spread out and we all walk faster. It's a long way to the spot where Greg parked. We plod down endless city streets. The hard cement hurts my feet and I don't think I can walk another block when we reach the van. Joel and I climb into the back seat. I lean my head on his shoulder and stretch my aching legs out as far as I can.

With all the cars on the road, it takes almost all night to get back to Isla Vista. Greg drives. The radio keeps him company while Joel and I doze, leaning against each other in the back seat of the bus. I'm exhausted from the long march after lying awake most of the night on the marina. Joel is asleep and I'm barely awake when Greg reaches back and slaps the top of Joel's head. "Wake up you guys—you gotta hear this!"

A familiar, ringing voice rails, "We in America are facing total peril!" Billy Graham, Nixon's evangelist buddy, has worked himself up into the rhythmic ranting that makes crowds get up out of their seats and come forward in droves at his "Crusades for Christ." He warns that all the antiwar protesters are dangerous radicals who are trying to take over the country and overthrow the American way of life. He accuses us of trying to plunge the whole country into a pit of moral decadence.

"Moral decadence is plenty good enough for me," Greg snickers. Joel laughs, but I'm chilled. My parents took me to three Billy Graham crusades and I've seen his hypnotic power over people. When he gets behind that pulpit, silence falls over the whole stadium as the huge audience strains to hear every single word. He points both fingers, shakes his fist, and swings his hand down in a chopping motion while he talks about sin and judgment. His voice has a hypnotic cadence that carries people along, and when he tells them to come forward, thousands rise up out of their seats and fill the aisles like zombies. It happens every time.

"You missed the *real* mind fuck," Greg says. "Get this—old Tricky Dick spent the day watching football on TV. There was a huge demonstration in Washington, even bigger than the one here, and he never even looked out the White House windows. It's as if we don't even fucking exist!"

It would be three more years before the United States pulled the troops out of Vietnam.

2

PICNICKING DOWN UNDER

I start the day with the best of intentions to get my assignments done. A paper is due comparing and contrasting world views expressed in Shelley's *Adonais* and Wordworth's *Ode: Intimations of Immortality,* and I haven't even started it yet. I make coffee and spread my books and notes out on the kitchen table. I sit down but instead of writing, I stare out the window. Students pass by on their way to their first classes. Some walk, others pedal by on bicycles.

Morning might not be a good time for this; my best writing pours out of me in the middle of the night when I'm hopped-up on Benzedrine or those little meth cross-tops truckers use; speed gives me glimpses into "the white radiance of eternity" in Shelley's poem.

A dark green VW bug with a yellow surfboard on top pulls up in front of our building. Joel! I jump up from the table and push the books into a pile. The buzzer makes a noise like an electric drill and I rush to open the door.

"Hi!" we both say at once, and we grin at each other like little kids. Joel stands on the porch, all in black rubber. The wetsuit clings to his body like a second skin—I try not to stare. His big feet are stuffed into a ragged pair of green tennis shoes. No laces. And me? Oh no—I'm still in the baggy navy blue T-shirt that I slept in. It barely covers my purple satin underpants. Not that he minds; he's checking out my legs.

"Wow—come on in!" I tug my shirt down. "I just made some coffee." What on earth is he doing in that wetsuit?

With a grin, Joel steps over the threshold. "You look cute in that shirt." He opens his arms. A smile bubbles up inside me and I step into them. We hug. The wetsuit's thick rubber keeps him separate from me, a full-body condom, only I can still feel him. "I couldn't wait to see you," he says. "It's so far out that you're here—I figured you'd be in class or something."

"I'm glad you came," I say.

"Me too." His arms tighten before we step apart.

I look him over, tilt my head to one side. "Uh… what's with the wetsuit?"

His smile turns shy and uncertain. "You're probably going to think this is crazy."

"Try me."

His next words spill out in a rush like jacks clattering onto the floor when you turn the bag upside down. "My roommate just told me about an illegal, private beach up the coast. I'm going to sneak in! Want to come? I mean, what an opportunity—the fuckin' beaches here are so crowded you have to fight to get a single wave. Imagine having a whole beach all to ourselves!"

"Uh… I'm not a surfer," I say.

He shrugs like it's no big deal. "I know that. But it'll be a beautiful, pristine beach. There'll be shells all over. You can wander around and explore while I surf."

Wow—He wants me there with him! "Outta sight!" I say. "I'll make some sandwiches."

The private, isolated beach is lonely and empty; the only signs of life on the long stretch of white sand are trails of bird tracks that crisscross like funny hieroglyphic messages. Joel lays his surfboard on the sand. He brought clothes to change into and fishes a square of surf wax out of the pocket of a pair of cutoffs. I shrug out of my pack. It's heavy with good things to eat: pastrami sandwiches, potato chips, juice, and oatmeal cookies. Joel kneels down and rubs wax on his board. A wave washes in all the way up to the board and recedes, leaving a conch shell behind. He picks it up and hands it to me.

"Nice one!" he says.

"Beautiful!" It's about four inches long, sparkly white.

"I'll surf for a while, and you can hunt for shells, explore—whatever you want to do. Then we'll have lunch."

"Okay."

After Joel paddles out, I sit on my towel in my cut-off jeans. Sandpipers scuttle back and forth along the shore. I hope the November sun will turn my legs a shade darker. Going out with a surfer gives me a whole new reason to be self-conscious. I have pale skin that doesn't tan easily. With other guys, my main worry was about whether I was thin enough. Out in the water, Joel catches a wave. He and the ocean dance together as he rides the wave in. Beautiful, such grace. He waves, his arm lifted high, then paddles out again.

We hike a steep, rocky path up the bluff that overlooks the beach. It's a hard slog. It's warm for November, and the early afternoon sun beats down on my shoulders and back and makes golden highlights in Joel's hair. With him ahead on the trail, we struggle uphill between clumps of scrub brush and parched, dry weeds. Joel, in ragged cutoff jeans and a white Hanes T-shirt, lugs his yellow surfboard along with our towels and his soggy wetsuit. My army surplus pack is getting heavier with every step—why hadn't I thought about this before I brought that half-gallon glass jug of apple juice? I packed too much lunch, too, and the leftover sandwiches, potato chips, and cookies compete for space with all the shells I've crammed into the pack. Conch shells, big sand dollars, periwinkles, scallops—I've never collected so many shells before. I work my thumbs under the unpadded pack straps where they dig into my shoulders and keep my eyes on Joel's surfboard just ahead of me. Oily tar blotches its fiberglass surface. No point in trying to clean it off, he says; the ocean is full of it. A sweaty strand of hair flops over my right eye and the weight of the pack settles back on my shoulders as I use my hands to twist my hair out of my face. My neck muscles ache from the constant pull, and my head is starting to throb.

At the top of the bluff, we halt. Joel sets his surfboard and wetsuit down in the weeds next to the big "No Trespassing" sign, and I take out the jug of apple juice. When I packed it, the juice was ice-cold. Now it's almost warm and sticky sweet, but it's liquid and we gulp it down. We pass it back and forth until we've drunk all of what's left in the bottle.

Joel wipes the back of his hand across his mouth and takes a last look at the beach far below. "What an awesome place. Too bad we can't come here all the time, but we were lucky we didn't get caught." He picks up his board and wraps the black wetsuit around it. I stuff the empty bottle into my pack. Not so heavy now; it feels a lot better when I slip it on.

Back on the path, we turn a corner and stop short. In the clearing there's a dusty green "California Department of Corrections" bus, and next to it sits a grizzle-haired black man in heavy work boots. He's balanced on a campstool and tends a fire in a pit surrounded by rocks. In the fire on a rack is an enormous metal coffee pot.

Joel's eyes bug out. "Wow—that was close! Just a little farther in, and they'd have seen us on that beach."

"Coffee almost ready," the man calls out. His gravelly deep voice rumbles with phlegm. He clears his throat and spits in the direction of the bus as we walk up to the fire. "Name's Thomas."

"Nice to meet you." Joel extends his hand. "I'm Joel, this is Kate." They shake hands.

"Ahhh, been enjoying the beach, I see." Thomas is ever so genial.

"Yep. Water's cold though, this time of year," Joel says. "You have a work crew here?"

"Oh, yeah, they clearing brush over yonder." He waves his hand, vaguely indicating somewhere north. "Gets lonely here—you'll stay for coffee?"

Joel looks at me and I nod. We sit down side by side on a log next to the path. "So, you fix food for the work crew?" I say.

"That's what I do. I'm the cook."

"How long have you been working for the prison system?" Joel asks.

"Twenty-seven years." It looks as if he has stuck to the same methods all that time, untouched by modernity, still boiling coffee the same way chuck wagon cooks did on the cattle drives in the old days. He's probably had that battered old coffee pot for twenty-seven years. Thomas gets up slowly. "I believe I've got some leftover cake." With slow, arthritic steps, he moseys over to the bus and hoists himself up into the vehicle.

"This is so surreal," I whisper to Joel. "Like we've gone back in time."

Joel stares at me, then he starts to smile. "I was thinking exactly the same thing. It's like we came up this path and found ourselves in the outback somewhere in Australia. Thomas could be one of those aboriginal guys boiling his billy can."

I look around. With the dry scrub brush everywhere, we really could be in Australia. "This is so trippy," I say. "First, San Francisco morphed into somewhere in Europe, and now all of a sudden, we're way down under."

"The adventure's still happening." His eyes have such a smile in them. He leans closer as if he's about to kiss me, but the bus door slams shut, interrupting the moment.

Thomas brings over a tin plate with slices of angel food cake and three tin cups. He takes one of the cups for himself. "Come on over and get yerselfs some coffee."

The boiled coffee is good, full of flavor. We need it to wash down the dry, stale cake.

"What kind of coffee is this?" I ask. "It's good."

"USDA surplus food commodity coffee—best there is. Comes in a big can."

Joel gets up. "I'll be right back. Got to go take a leak."

"You be careful," Thomas warns. "They killed a snake over there. Them heads can still bite."

"Okay. Thanks for the heads-up." Joel grins at me and rolls his eyes once he's behind Thomas's back.

"How do you make coffee like this?" I ask Thomas. "I've got one of those pots where you pour the water in and let it drip through, and my coffee doesn't taste anything like this."

"Well, you scoop a cup of dry coffee for a pot this size. Then you fill the pot with cold water—make sure it's cold. You bring it to a slow boil and let it simmer for about ten minutes. After that, just keep it warm."

Joel comes back, walking fast. "Kate—you want to see something *really* surreal, come look at this!"

I follow him into the brush on the other side of the path. Thomas trails behind us. There in the dirt lies the body of a grayish-brown rattlesnake, about three feet long. A row of solid brown markings runs down its back, outlined by white in a diamond pattern. Both ends of the snake are bloody stumps; its head and rattles have been chopped off, but still the snake coils and uncoils as if it's alive. Its three-inch-wide, triangular head lies next to a chunk of granite about ten feet away. What in the world?

Joel stares at the snake, then back at me. He opens his hands and widens his eyes; he might as well be saying, "Don't ask me—I have no idea."

The snake displaces bits of sand and gravel as it moves. Soon it will be coiling itself on smooth dirt.

"Isn't that the weirdest thing you ever saw?" Joel says.

"This is so bizarre! How can it be moving around like that? It should be dead." I look at Thomas. Maybe he knows.

Thomas shrugs. "That snake be searching for his head. He *know* it got to be around here somewhere."

Watching the dead snake's sad, futile search makes me sad, too. I hate the way people kill snakes. A rattlesnake won't bother you if you just stand back and let it go on its way. Daddy used to catch non-poisonous snakes in the woods and let them go down the holes gophers made in our lawn, but before he released them, he'd bring them inside to show me. I would hold them and feel how cool and smooth they were. Most people hate snakes, but I was brought up to love them. Maybe because of the way they glide along without legs, as if by magic, they feel sacred to me.

The rattlesnake twists and turns, side to side, back and forth, never pausing in its endless motion, the headless stump reaching, searching. I can't take my eyes away. The motion sucks me down through a tear in reality into some other place, a dark eternity of despair like a horrible dream, like hell.

"He'll keep movin' 'til sundown," Thomas says.

"Probably some kind of nerve and muscle reaction," Joel guesses. "But it's unbelievably creepy."

My eyes are glued to the snake as the awful writhing continues; I can't move.

Joel tugs my hand, bringing me out of my daze. He slips his arm around my shoulders. "Come on." He guides me back to the fire.

Thomas pours us each a second cup of coffee and we all sit without speaking. We take slow sips of the hot, rich brew. Beyond us where the snake is, the rip in the air comes back together and seals shut. We're safe. I don't notice how my shoulder muscles are clenched into hard knots until I feel them loosen and let go. I roll my neck from side to side. Ahhhh. Feels good.

"Let me wash these cups," I say when we're done.

"Naw—prisoners got to do the dishes." Thomas sets our cups in a dented enamel dishpan under the bus.

The floor mats in the VW bug are gritty with dirt and sand. A dried coffee stain streaks the dashboard. Joel throws the towels and wetsuit onto the back seat and I put my pack in next to them. We get in, slam the doors. I stretch out my legs and feel my body sink into the warm upholstery. Joel digs in his pocket for keys, turns the key in the ignition, and the bug purrs into life. "Jesus—was that weird or what?" He turns and gives me a disbelieving look, brows lowered, eyes intense. "It was almost like being on acid—only, we're totally straight!"

"Yeah, can you imagine if we'd just smoked a doobie?"

Joel puts the bug in gear. With a deep, growly laugh, he pulls out onto the highway.

"What?" I say.

"We weren't stoned at the moratorium either, but we keep having these mind-blowing adventures."

"That's because we've both got great imaginations," I say.

"This is true. And our imaginations seem to work the same way." He lays his hand on my knee for a moment, then grabs the gearshift and takes the car up to fourth.

The VW eats up the miles; Joel must be going eighty at least. I steal glances at his brown hands and the easy way they hold the steering wheel. My fingers ache to trace the veins coursing down his lean forearms. Is he ever going to make a move? Or did the dead snake ruin any chance of that?

It was so horrid the way they chopped off the rattles, like a trophy. Daddy shoots hawks and chops off their taloned feet. He's got a whole collection. I love the way he taught me to like snakes, but I hate the way he kills birds—

"Wait!" Joel bangs the wheel with his hand. "What the fuck am I doing, flooring it like we're late to some crisis or something! I don't want to go back yet."

Yes, yes, yes! I wiggle my toes and press them into the floor mat, happy. "Neither do I," I say, and we grin at each other. Joel takes his foot off the accelerator and the car begins to slow. He downshifts and pulls off the highway onto the next side road. We drive past pine woods, then park on a bluff that overlooks a cobalt blue sea dotted with whitecaps. Light shimmers on the surface of the water; the sparkles wink in and out with the pulse of the incoming waves, as if the ocean were breathing. We get out of the car. Joel laces his fingers with mine as we walk to the edge of the bluff. Cormorants with wingspans like black eagles swoop and dive into the waves.

"Must be a school of fish out there—look at that!" Joel points. One of the giant birds comes up with a fish in its beak and flies away from the others, toward the rocks.

"Far out!" I say. "I didn't know whether any of them were left." So many cormorants and other shore birds died in the Santa Barbara channel oil spill earlier this year.

Joel steps behind me and slides his hands up under my shirt and inside my bra. I lean up against him, melt into him. I reach behind and work my fingers into his back pockets; tug him closer still. Our cheeks touch. His feels rough. He sinks his nose into my neck and kisses my cheek once. "Come on," he breathes into my ear.

"Yes," I whisper.

Still leaning against each other, bumping shoulders, we get the towels out of the car. Joel slings them over his arm and we head for the woods. Hand in hand, we pick our way among the trees through tall, weedy grass. We come to an open spot under a pine tree. He squeezes my hand. "Here?"

I nod. "Yeah, this is good."

We spread the towels over slippery pine needles. We kick off our shoes and step onto the soft terrycloth. I put my hands on his shoulders and he strokes his fingers down my sides. Then he's holding my waist. His arms slide up my back and he pulls me in close. My hands slip off his shoulders and trail down his back. I pull up the bottom of his shirt and slip my fingers underneath. His skin is smooth and hot. We sway in a slow dance in time with the ocean waves. Cormorants in the distance call to each other, their deep squawks wild and jubilant. A piney smell rises as the weight of our feet stirs the fallen needles and crushes them. Joel lets go of me and pulls off his white T-shirt. I suck in my breath. Now comes the moment of truth. *Playboy* isn't going to be recruiting me any time soon. But he has to know that already. I shrug out of my sleeveless blouse and unhook my size 34-A bra. He slides the straps down over my shoulders and cups my breasts in his hands as I run my fingers over his chest and flat belly. I pull him close and bury my face in his neck. He smells like saltwater with a hint of wetsuit rubber. I taste him. Salty. Warm. We step out of our shorts and kick them aside. Now he pulls me down next to him on the towel and kisses my forehead, my nose, my cheeks. His salty-smelling hair drags across my face. His tongue tickles my cheek before his lips meet mine at last, and we kiss deep and long. The cries of the cormorants blend into the kiss, and it is as if we become those birds. We gaze into each other's eyes as we move, flying slowly at first. The smile in his eyes melts and becomes soft and unfocused as we lose ourselves in the wildness of coming together. Faster now, swooping over the sea, we roll over and over, off the towels onto pine needles that give way to soft, bare earth underneath us.

Afterwards, we lie in the dirt, gazing into each other's eyes. Joel strokes my hair and picks out two pine needles. "This is meaning a lot more than I thought it would," he says.

Did he really say that? I'm not used to that kind of openness. I stroke a smudge of black earth off his left cheekbone. "Yes, for me too," I whisper. It's our first time, but it doesn't feel like that at all. It feels like we have known each other all our lives.

"Ha—look at us. We really ground ourselves into the dirt, didn't we?" Eyes half closed, lips upturned, he is the picture of wicked satisfaction.

"Yeah," I say. "Kind of a reverse baptism."

We burst out laughing.

3

THINGS WE NEVER EXPECTED

I use an orange pencil to print "768" on the sheet of butcher paper spread out on the kitchen table. That was the year Charlemagne became king of the Carolingians, the German dynasty that ruled most of Western Europe. Joel and I sit next to each other at the table with a bottle of Hansen's Natural Apple Juice and big mugs of tea. He has the book and I have the pencils to map out a time line to help me prepare for my history final two days from now.

"Okay," Joel says, and turns a page in the big red-orange book, *History of Western Civilization, Volume II.* "Now put the year 800, when he got crowned Roman Emperor by Pope Leo III."

I use the same pencil. Orange, a mixture of red and gold, is a good color for Charlemagne. The name makes me think of a lion, thick-maned and muscular, like Joel, who just happens to be a Leo. King Otto I, farther down the line at 962, is blue. Popes are red. As we work, it has gotten dark and the kitchen window is night black now. Our reflections in the glass make it look like there's another room beyond this one. What if that room is the real one, and we're just reflections? We'll never know...

Under the table, I slide my bare foot across the green linoleum and nudge Joel's foot. I wiggle my toes. His foot pounces and pins mine down. His foot is like a warm blanket enveloping my chilly toes. He pretends to be engrossed in the book but gives me a wicked sideways glance, the corners of his lips turned up like a cat's mouth. My foot pretends to struggle, but it doesn't try very hard.

"You think Charlemagne played footsies?" I say.

"No way, girl," Joel says. He looks up from the book and rolls his eyes at me. "Men and women didn't play with each other. You're lucky to be living now—chicks had to wear chastity belts in those days. They didn't have sex for fun."

I pick up my mug of tea and take a sip. It's my favorite, Earl Grey, citrus rind with a hint of menthol. The fragrance is like strolling through an herb garden on a sunny day—heavenly. "You're probably right," I say. The popes though... sex was definitely not okay for them. It was forbidden, taboo, so *they* couldn't get enough. Nuns, other priests, young girls, altar boys, sheep, goats..." I dissolve in helpless giggles.

Joel scoots his chair closer until our arms touch. "I'm going to get a red nightshirt," he growls. "It'll be my pope robe. When I do, you'd better watch out."

"Mmmmm. Pope Leo." I lean my head on his shoulder. "I had no idea doing a time line could be so much fun! History the way it's written is so boring. Tedious. It's torture."

Joel takes a gulp from the bottle of Hansen's apple juice. His Adam's apple goes up and down as he swallows. "Really? I think this time line idea is kinda cool."

I pick up Charlemagne's orange pencil and doodle a sunflower on the edge of the paper. "Yeah, but all they tell about is power shifting back and forth between the popes and emperors. Where are all the regular people?"

"Oh, you mean serfs?" He sets down the empty bottle. "They kinda left them out of the books, didn't they?"

"Yeah. What was it like for them in the ninth century?" I nuzzle my face into his neck, then look at the time line again.

"To the pope, everybody would be a serf," he says. "There weren't any newspapers—nobody would have had a clue about all the shoving back and forth going on at the top. They'd go to mass, believing it was about God, but the church wasn't any different from the emperor—they were all overlords... That's why Karl Marx called religion 'the opium of the people.'"

I press my palms over my eyes. I've been studying all day. Time lines do help me see the whole picture at once, but I don't like the big picture. It's too familiar. Young people, poor people don't exist for the Nixon administration any more than the peasants did for the pope and the Holy Roman Emperor, except as draft fodder. We don't really have much more of a voice than the serfs did.

I tap the history textbook with my pen. "You know—it would be way more interesting from a different approach," I say. "Look at Tolkien. *Everybody's* read the *Lord of the Rings*, and that was *long!* It was crammed with the history Tolkien made up for his Middle Earth world, which was really medieval. But we all stayed glued to the very end because we cared about the *people* in the middle of that history. A lot of cats and dogs around here are named Gandalf, Baggins, Frodo..."

"Fuck yes!" Joel sets the open book on the table and turns toward me, his eyes bright with excitement. "It's the mythology of our time. Frodo is the hero, maybe the last hero we've got now that they've killed Bobby Kennedy and Martin Luther King."

I lean my elbow on the table and put my chin in my hand. Things would be so different now if Bobby and Dr. King were still here. Nixon wouldn't be President. "I know—and we're all hunkered down like hobbits with the police hassling everybody, illegally searching and busting people all the time. Like the dark riders of Mordor."

"Nazgul." He spits out the word for those dark riders. "And the war and the draft sure do play into it all."

"Yeah." I tug a long, dark strand of hair forward, hold it in front of my face, and examine it for split ends the way I always do when I'm uneasy. I see a couple before I let go of the strand. All the shampoos and cream rinses promise to mend split ends, but none of them do jack shit. "The thing is," I say, "There's been a crucial change since Charlemagne's time. The king led his troops into battle himself. He didn't send people out to die while he stayed holed up in the palace watching football games the way our leaders do now."

"God—I never thought of it that way. That's really heavy." Joel scratches his forehead and stares at our reflections in the window. Then he scoots his chair forward and picks up the book. "Let's hurry up and get this thing done," he says. "Then we can go over to my place; I've got steaks we can broil."

"Really? Far out!" I say, although I kind of wish he'd brought the meat here. Joel and his roommates are real slobs when it comes to housekeeping.

Joel turns the page. "Okay. The next one is 1085—Heinrich IV attacks Italy and drives the pope out of Rome."

I make that one purple.

A row of mailboxes stands at the top of the driveway under the stairwell. Joel stops, opens his mailbox, and pulls out several envelopes that he tucks under his arm before we climb the stairs to the top floor apartment he shares with two other guys, Greg and Dan. He pulls a key out of his pocket, unlocks the door, and flips the light switch. He has a spacious living room with a big sliding glass door that opens onto a balcony that overlooks the beach. The apartment is messier than ever. Nobody has vacuumed since the guys moved in at the start of the term. The blue carpet is gritty with tracked-in sand and dirt. It crunches when I walk across it. Surfboards lie on the floor and turn the room into an obstacle course, and textbooks, old mail, and fast food wrappers are scattered on every surface, the coffee table, the sofa, even the stereo. Taped-up posters decorate the walls— "Light My Fire" in pink, purple, and orange with a couple making love amidst flames; Rasputin; Bob Dylan; and "Zappa Crappa—" Frank Zappa sitting on a toilet. It's cold in here. I wrap my arms around myself and shiver. The glass balcony door has been left open and the ocean air has blown away the stuffy, stale smell that was here the last time I visited. Joel sets his mail on the counter between the living room and kitchen, strides to the balcony, and yanks the door shut. He turns up the thermostat dial on the wall under the Zappa poster. "Should be warm in a few minutes."

The narrow kitchen has a grease-spattered stove at one end. Joel tugs open the fridge door. He takes out a jug of Gallo Rose, two steaks packed in saran wrap, a box of Bird's Eye frozen mixed vegetables, butter, and a bottle of Worchestershire sauce. I squat down on the sticky linoleum floor, pull a pan out of one of the bottom cupboards, set it on a burner, and get started melting butter for the mixed vegetables.

The pile of dirty dishes in the sink is stacked so high that one more plate could start an avalanche. Joel checks the cupboards. "Shit.

Got to wash some dishes or we won't have any plates." He turns on the water, picks up a can of Ajax cleanser, sprinkles the white powder on one of the dirty plates and goes at it with a wet paper towel. I set the butter down. What on earth?

"Is that all you have to do dishes with?"

"Huh?" He turns, eyes wide. His mouth drops open. "What do you mean?"

"That's not for washing dishes," I say. "It's for scrubbing sinks and toilets, stuff like that."

"Oh." His eyebrows shoot up as he looks at the can in his hand. "How was I supposed to know? It says 'Cleanser.'" He holds the can up and shakes it. White powder spills out on the pile of dirty dishes.

It's obvious Joel and his friends never washed a dish in their lives until they left home. "There's dish soap specially for that," I say. "I'll get you some next time I go to the store. It'll make it a whole lot easier."

I tear open the Birds Eye box and upend it; the frozen vegetables clatter into the pan and sizzle when they hit the hot butter. I sprinkle in some Lawry's seasoned salt. I pick up a roll of aluminum foil on the counter next to the stove and tear off two sheets. I fold the sides to make shallow trays for the meat and turn on the broiler.

Joel holds the plates under the faucet to rinse off the gritty cleanser. "Shit. Paper plates would be a lot easier."

I shove a towel and sweatshirt to one side to clear a space on the counter and wipe it down with more paper towels. Joel washes two juice glasses and pours the wine. I slide the steaks under the broiler and stir the vegetables to keep them from sticking.

Joel hands me a glass of wine. "I want to show you something," he says, "Dan's entrepreneurial venture."

He leads the way down a hall with three bedrooms and a bathroom. Dan's room is at the end. Propped on every available surface—the desk, bed, and chair—are identical, half-finished watercolor paintings of the ocean. "He does a whole batch at once, like an assembly line," Joel explains. "He calls them 'Wave and Sky' and sells them at the surf shop. He's sold a shitload already."

They're pretty, but there's nothing exciting about them. The colors are serene shades of blue. "Wow!" I say. "He's got his own little factory here." The aroma of meat cooking drifts down the hall. "Oh—gotta flip those steaks over."

We let the steaks broil a little longer, then Joel forks them onto our plates and sprinkles them with Worchestershire sauce. I spoon out a big helping of vegetables for each of us and we hoist ourselves up on the bar stools at the counter.

"So how did Dan get the idea of mass-producing watercolors?" I take a bite of buttery veggies and the MSG-enhanced flavors explode on my tongue.

"He took photos of different surf spots that guys will recognize and copied them over and over until he had his technique down. He paints each little bit on all the pictures, then goes on to the next bit."

I grin. "Kind of like paint by number?"

"Yeah. He ends up with five or six all done at the same time; he has it down to a science. He clears about ten bucks apiece—he'll never even have to get a job!" Joel cuts off the end of his steak, swabs up sauce on his plate, and crams it into his mouth.

"Hmmmmm." I swallow my bite of steak and take a sip of wine. "He's gonna have to get more stores to carry his stuff. He'll run out of buyers with just that one local surf shop."

Joel picks up his mail and starts leafing through it. "He probably will. He's smart... What? Something from the university?" He tears open the envelope and unfolds the sheet of paper inside. His mouth falls open and he jerks his head back. "Oh, FUCK!"

"What happened? What is it?" I jump off my stool and get behind him to look over his shoulder.

"Shit—look at this." He holds the paper up so I can see it. "I'm fucked."

It's a letter on official-looking stationery: "Dean of Students, University of California, Santa Barbara" is at the top. Centered underneath in capital letters, it says: "NOTICE OF EXPULSION." It goes on to say "Pursuant to the fact that you have failed to complete your assignments thus far in a timely manner, your student privileges are hereby revoked..."

I take the paper out of his hand and squint at it. This has to be a mistake. "Whoa," I say. "What kind of bullshit is this?" I put the letter on the counter with the rest of his mail and reach for my wine glass.

"I haven't done diddly squat this semester," he says. "I figured they'd just give me an incomplete though, and I could make it up later. But this—talk about a major mind fuck!" He gets off his stool and grabs the wine bottle on the counter next to the sink.

I spin around and face him. I can't believe this. "Wait a minute! You haven't done any work? Are you serious?"

His lips droop and get pouty. "I didn't feel like it. I just wanted to surf, and be with you." He sloshes more wine into his glass and takes it to the end of the counter. He scowls down at the letter, then looks at me, his eyes direct. "Believe me, I didn't expect this."

My breath whooshes out in a loud sigh. "Oh *shit*—does this mean you have to leave?"

"Not yet." He scratches the side of his nose. "Rent's paid through January."

I get back on my stool. While I think, I use my fork to separate my veggies into piles of carrot chunks, peas, and corn.

Joel sits on the stool next to me. "What are you thinking?" he asks.

"I don't want you to leave." I burst out.

He slips his arm around my shoulder and pulls me close. Our cheeks touch. "Awwww...." He says.

An idea pops into my mind. "I know—You could paint surf pictures like Dan!"

He shakes his head. "Nah, I couldn't draw my way out of a paper bag. My fine motor coordination sucks. You've seen my handwriting."

It's true. Joel's writing is terrible, a childlike, illegible chicken scratch. He hacks off another chunk of meat, crams it into his mouth, and grinds it between his teeth. He drains his cup of wine.

An ache starts in my chest and moves up into my throat. I don't feel like eating anymore. I set my fork down and stare across the counter at the mess in the living room. What's going to happen to us?

His hand slips around my back. He strokes my shoulder. "Hey, it'll be okay. C'mon, eat your dinner."

"But what're you going to *do*?" I pick up my fork and mix the veggies back together, but no way can I eat.

Joel wolfs down the rest of his food while he thinks. "God knows—I have no idea," he says. "I really didn't see this coming... But for now, let's finish eating and go back to your place." He laces his fingers together and pushes outward. His knuckles make businesslike little pops. "I'll bet a thousand bucks the same letter is sitting at my parents' house. I don't want to be here when they open it!"

"Okay," I say. "I'm ready. I can't eat anymore." I swallow the rest of the wine in my glass.

"Ahhhh—at least eat *some*. Tell you what—we'll eat it together." His fork snakes over to my plate and scoops up a bite of veggies.

I try another bite of steak. It's tender and juicy, medium rare the way I like it. I push the plate over so it's right between us, and he smiles. We skooch our barstools together. In between bites, I rest my head on his shoulder. His hair brushes my face as he slices off a chunk of meat. His breath smells like wine and Worchestershire sauce. Between us, we clean my plate in no time.

Joel calls me as soon as his parents leave. I pick up the phone in the kitchen. His folks were so angry that they drove up to Isla Vista and demanded a refund on January's rent. They were going to move him out and take him home right then, but the property management company's "no refunds" policy, the way they bilk the students out of every possible cent turned out to be a good thing for once. "I get to stay until the end of January," he tells me.

"Wow—what a relief!" I say. I move the phone from the kitchen counter to the table so I can collapse into one of the metal chairs. I twist the cord around my fingers.

"Yeah, but after that, it's going to be really fucked," he says. My mom pulled strings and got me a job in the mail room at the Department of Water and Power where she works. I'll have to get a haircut and *everything!*"

January is almost over. I walk out of my last class in North Hall. My leather sandals make a hollow, echoing sound on the concrete corridor. Other people hurry past but I feel as if I'm the last person on earth. There's a heavy ache in my chest and my throat is tight—only two more days before Joel has to leave. Tears start and my vision gets all blurry, but I'm not looking where I'm going anyway. All this time, Joel has been pretending he'll be here forever, but now the awful reality of his situation has sunk in. Both of us cried last night. We didn't make love, we just held each other and sobbed.

I hate this, and I hate the way I'm falling apart. I need to be brave and strong for Joel—after all, *he's* the one who has to leave this beautiful place and go back to LA. I start across the quadrangle in front of the administration building and take a few steps before I even notice the crowd. A wall of people, shoulder to shoulder—I've stumbled into a demonstration. An antiwar rally? I swipe my arm across my eyes and look around. The crowd shouts "Open hearing! Open hearing!" Oh... The university just fired Bill Allen, a very popular anthropology professor. Over seven thousand people, more than half the student body, signed a petition for an open hearing of the case. I signed it myself; fair is fair. I've never taken his class and know next to nothing about the guy, but solidarity matters, so I stay. I try to push down my sadness—I can cry later. Late afternoon sun streams over us and casts long shadows across the pavement. The lawn bordering the square is a warm, sleepy green, and I remember sitting on the grass next to Joel at the moratorium, where he kissed me for the first time... Phil Ochs was singing but we weren't listening; all our attention was on each other. I stand in the crowd, lost in a daydream.

"Clear the area! This is an unlawful gathering—" blasts out of a bullhorn while police in helmets and gas masks converge on us from all sides. A loud pop explodes over my head, and tear gas sears my eyes and burns down my throat. Dull thuds of hard wood hitting flesh make a sickening sound as the police swing their clubs at anyone within striking distance. Shrieks and screams everywhere almost drown out the bullhorn. A girl trips and falls as she tries to swerve away from one policeman's club. A cop with masking tape over his badge yanks the glasses off a guy with a camera five feet from me, drops them on the ground, and stomps on them.

I clutch my books and run like a spooked horse until I reach the library. Students talk and joke as they unlock their bicycles and wheel them out of the metal racks. It's so ordinary it's surreal. I want to shout, "Don't you know the police are beating the crap out of people?" But instead, I slow to a walk and do my best to look casual as I leave the campus in case any cops have followed me. I swipe my arm across my sweaty forehead. I've been lugging my books under my left arm and I switch them to the right. I wipe my moist left hand on my jeans. My nose runs and my eyes are still burning.

On the streets, nothing has changed; cars and bicycles cruise by, and people go in and out of the little shops. The Rexall drugstore where I get my birth control pills is still intact on the corner. I remember that night last fall when the "Travel Agency" band set up their drum kit and amplifiers in the Rexall parking lot. We danced for hours. It had been a hot day and even though night had fallen, the asphalt was still warm.

Back at my apartment, I throw myself down on the squishy couch cushions. I'm reeling. The police are supposed to get out their bullhorns and give a warning before they attack people. Did they really just wade in with their clubs? And what was the masking tape on their badges all about? I was right there, but I can't believe it happened. I kick off my shoes, push off the sofa and pad across the dingy beige carpet to the bathroom. I lean my hands on the edge of the washbasin. In the mirror, my face looks blotchy. My cheeks are flushed and my nose is all red. My eyes are puffy and bloodshot. It happened, all right. I blow my nose; there's blood in the snot from the tear gas. I splash cold water in my face and eyes again and again.

4

A WHOLE NIGHT'S WORTH OF GOODBYES

It looks like the "Big One," the long-predicted, catastrophic earthquake, just happened in here. Towels, wetsuit, shoes, and dirty socks litter the floor. Sheets and blankets spill off the side of Joel's bed. We cram jeans, shirts, swimming trunks and underwear straight from his messy drawers into a big suitcase. We don't have time to sort anything because Joel waited until the last minute to pack. We stuff records, books, and Surfer magazines into cardboard boxes. I pack the green glass water pipe and his bongo drums into another carton. Packing his things gives me a hollow ache in my throat and chest. No more nights passing that pipe back and forth before we make love, no more Crosby, Stills and Nash...

Joel yanks the sheets off the bed and stuffs them into the pillowcase. I fold the blanket and lay it on the bare mattress. He grabs a box to carry out, and I follow him with the suitcase.

He stops in the living room. "Wait a minute," he says, and sets the box on the couch.

I put the suitcase down. Joel steps out on the balcony to look at the ocean, one hand lifted to shade his eyes from the late afternoon sun, sniffing the air like a wolf. His long, sun-bleached hair falls over muscular brown shoulders and hangs down his back. I suck in my breath and swallow to clear the sudden catch in my throat. I'll never see that gorgeous hair again. It'll be gone the next time I see him, lying on some barbershop floor.

Joel turns away from the ocean and comes back inside. "Waves are pissy today." Lucky for me—if the surf was good, I might end up doing all the packing myself. He strides back to the sofa and grabs the box. We carry our load downstairs and Joel stuffs the box and suitcase into the back seat of the Bug. We head back up to get more of his things.

At last the bedroom is empty. I pick up bits of discarded mail and Joel crams old dirty white socks into a brown paper trash bag.

"Don't you want your socks?" I ask.

"Nah, I'll just get new ones."

I think about salvaging them, sticking them in with my own laundry, but I'm worn out.

We look around the room one last time. Nothing is left; we're done.

"Let's go get some pizza," Joel says.

"Oh yeah! I'm starving." I can almost taste the melted cheese and warm, spicy tomato sauce.

Joel's boots thud on the scuffed gray wooden steps and drown out the soft slip of my sandals. I'm going to miss the clomp-clomp of his boots that always lets me know he's coming. He gets in the Bug's driver's seat and leans over to unlock the door on the passenger side for me. I get in. The upholstery feels gritty and spilled sand crunches under my feet. I take my hairbrush out of my purse and tug it through my hair.

"Let me use that for a second," Joel says when I'm done.

I grin and hand him the brush. "Hey—remember that morning in San Francisco when you borrowed my hairbrush?"

"Shit. I come out of the bus and there's you and I'm trying to bum a hairbrush like one of those people going 'spaaarre changgge?' I wasn't awake yet. A minute later I'm going O shit. What must she *think*?" He gives his hair a quick going over.

"I was just glad there was somebody to talk to. I'd spent the whole night being scared shitless. But then I put my hand up to my head and realized my own hair was a complete rat's nest. Then it was me going O shit."

We grin at each other and laughter explodes out of us both at the same time. "Like my hair looked any better," he says. He gives my arm a playful shove.

"It did," I say. "Trust me. I think I was already starting to have a thing for you."

"Awww darlin', that's sweet." He hands the brush back and turns the key in the ignition. The radio comes on; it's Linda Ronstadt singing "Long, Long Time." [1]

"Oh God," Joel says. "This song always brings tears to my eyes." We listen a moment, then he swipes the back of his hand across his eyes and pulls the car out of the driveway.

Mama's has the best pizza in Santa Barbara. We sit on opposite sides of a little table for two with a red and white checked tablecloth. I take a book of matches out of my purse and light the blue candle in one of those chianti bottles wrapped in straw. It flickers between us and gives his skin a golden glow. A waiter brings the pizza and sets it on a circular metal stand in the center of the table. He moves the candle over to the side. The pizza is gorgeous—thick, bubbly mozzarella cheese studded with chunks of Italian sausage and fat mushroom slices. We lift big pieces onto our plates. Mmmmmm, thick chewy crust, like fresh-baked Italian bread. For a long time we don't speak. We just savor big juicy bites. It's not something you can nibble at—it's the sort of food you inhale. It's "died and gone to heaven" pizza.

Joel and I walk on the beach afterwards; he's brought a blanket and I carry a bottle of Japanese plum wine. Hand in hand, we stroll at the edge of the water. Warm waves splash over our bare feet. We go far from the beach stairs; then he lets go of my hand and slips his arm around my shoulder. We turn away from the water and pick our way toward the cliffs between clumps of tar and ropes of seaweed. Together, we spread the blanket out on a patch of soft, dry sand. Underneath the salty smell from the ocean, there's a faint whiff of petroleum. Oil platforms dot the Santa Barbara channel—ugly, metal structures that look like erector sets looming up out of the ocean, but at night, when they're lit up, they become palaces. The oil company gave them names like Henry, Grace, and Gilda. The one standing sentinel in the water off Isla Vista is named Holly, but we call it the

Crystal Ship. It's lit up like a fairy castle, and the light from it makes a sparkling path across the water. Joel and I sit down on the blanket and he opens the plum wine. We lean against each other and gaze out over the water. He hands me the bottle and I take a long swig. It's sweet and the warmth goes all the way down to my stomach.

"I really fucking don't want to leave," Joel says. "I can't believe my parents are making me move back in with them!"

"I don't know what I'll do without you." I say. I don't have a bit of trouble believing it—if UCSB kicked me out, my parents would probably march me over to the Army recruitment center and I'd be a WAC before I knew what was happening. But Joel just does whatever he pleases. He doesn't seem to believe in consequences. I hate the way he just shined on his classes to surf whenever the waves were good, but at the same time, I adore him for having the guts to do what he wants, even though he's paying for it now, big time. Not only does he have to go live with his parents; getting kicked out of school has ended his student protection from the draft. He could die.

I screw the top back on the wine bottle and it rolls to the side as I turn to face him, grab his shoulders and bury my face in his grubby tee-shirt. My tears well up and leak into the soft cotton.

He hugs me hard. "Oh, Darling—I'll never leave you! I'll come back to you every weekend." We fall over and he rolls on top of me. He kneels up to pull his shirt off. He smiles down at me and pushes my T-shirt up. I'm not wearing anything underneath. "Mmmm, better," he says, but my back is arched over the wine bottle.

"Just a minute," I say. I lift up and yank it out from under me. I tug my shirt all the way off while I'm at it and sink back down. We gaze at each other. Now he's the one with tears in his eyes. I wrap my arms around him, so tight, and intertwine my legs with his. I undo his belt buckle, unfasten his Levis, and work my fingers into the belt loops. I push the pants down toward his feet. He rolls off me and yanks them off, first the right leg, then the left. I'm undoing my own pants but he pushes my hands aside and tugs them off himself. Now we're naked under the stars, rolling over and over, him on top, then me. The ocean rushes in, then rolls back in its endless rhythm. Out on the water, the Crystal Ship sparkles and glows.

It's past time for Joel to leave. We've said a whole night's worth of goodbyes on the beach and later in my bed. Now it's early morning and the Bug is waiting in the driveway. I want it to wait forever, to sit there until the tires disintegrate and all that's left is a rusted metal carcass, but instead I walk out with him and we hug one last time. Joel pops the trunk and paws through the boxes crammed into the small space. He pulls out a record album—Crosby, Stills, and Nash. "I want you to have this, so you don't forget me between weekends." It was the music he always put on when we made love in his beachfront apartment. His face is grave, serious.

"Like I would ever forget you." I hug the record to my chest. "I'll probably wear it out by the time you come back."

The first days without him are the worst. I play that Crosby, Stills and Nash album over and over, lonely and horny. I go to my classes but they're a blur; I'm just marking time until the weekend. It takes days before I can concentrate on my schoolwork again. What I can't seem to avoid, though, is the unrest over the university firing Bill Allen and the police brutality that went with it. It's all people talk about. In spite of the petition and the crowds of students who marched and demonstrated, the university refused to hold an open hearing of the case. Not only does Nixon ignore the antiwar demonstrations, the university ignores the students. We don't have a voice at all. An angry undercurrent festers in the student union, in the lecture halls, and in the coffeehouses and bookstores. I feel it, but it gets shoved to the back of my mind, behind worries about Joel. Will he forget about me? Will the drive to Isla Vista turn into a tiresome chore? How long will it be until he meets someone else?

5

SOMETHING'S BURNING

It's a windy February afternoon. The stadium is packed; William Kunstler, the attorney for the Chicago Seven, activists charged with conspiracy to start a riot during the Democratic convention, is here. I sit near the top of the metal bleachers and look down across a sea of heads at the podium on the football field below. Kunstler is handsome, older but a real fox. He fiddles with the microphone. The wind musses his long brown hair. He begins to speak. He holds up a Chicago newspaper with a huge headline, "Kunstler Visit Sparks Riot" that he picked up at the airport this morning before boarding his flight to California. "They were a little early, because I hadn't come yet."[1] The conspiracy charges against his clients are trumped up too; he explains why the government wanted each one of them. They're being used as examples to put fear into people, make them afraid to get involved. The way he lambastes the universities and the whole justice system has everybody clapping and yelling "Right on!" I clap until my hands hurt.

After the speech, there's going to be a rally in Perfect Park. We file out of the stadium and walk down Stadium Road toward Isla Vista. Patrol cars speed across the grass toward the crowd. In front of everybody, the police gang up on a black man with a bottle of wine. Like a frenzied pack of wild dogs, they beat him again and again with their clubs. Either they haven't noticed that hundreds of people are watching, or they don't care. Hardly anyone shows up for the rally.

Instead, there's a rampage. Students smash windows at the slumlord property management offices. Somebody overturns a police car and sets it on fire. On my way home, I pick my way through broken glass and skirt around the rioting mob with their rocks and lengths of pipe. Gandhi and Martin Luther King are my heroes—this sort of violent backlash isn't going to help at all—it'll just make everything worse. At the same time, though, I'm thrilled. I can't help it. That burning police car fills me with a grim satisfaction. After they beat up that man and the way they're always lurking to bust people for drugs— they even plant stashes when their searches fail to turn up anything— I just can't help feeling they're getting theirs. I walk home holding my head a little higher.

I hate that Joel isn't here. If he hadn't flunked out, we would've heard Kunstler's speech together. We'd be discussing everything he said and whether we should join the rioters. Kunstler didn't approve of breaking windows, but he didn't condemn it either. But Joel is in LA with his parents, working the swing shift in an office, shorn of his lion's mane of hair, wearing "straight" business clothes, feeling sorry for himself. Every Friday night after work, he drives back to Isla Vista and we're inseparable until Sunday night. Then he has to go back, and I'm alone for five long days.

I walk up our duplex driveway—I can hardly wait to talk to June, my roommate, but the apartment is empty. It's always like this— every time I really need someone, I can count on being alone. I feel like I'm always waiting. My last boyfriend, Daniel, went away for the summer and never came back to UCSB. Before that, Ramon went to Germany. Now Joel is gone. My throat gets all scratchy and tears overflow. I swipe my arm across my eyes and stumble into the kitchen where the phone sits on the cracked avocado green Formica counter. I call Joel's number, my longing more intense with each turn of the dial. But his mom answers. "Oh, he already left for work." The cheap metal kitchen table chairs with their green vinyl seats are empty. In the living room, the velveteen brown sofa is a scowling, unwelcoming hulk underneath the window. A dead fly lies on the sill. Even the purple paisley cushions in the cozy pillow corner mock me. "You're all alone. You always end up alone."

The beige carpet is dingy with ground-in dirt and sand, except for one spot in the middle where June and I, high on hash, explored the tactile sensation of rubbing soap from an overturned bottle of bubble-blowing liquid into the fibers. The lush bubbles foamed up and slid through our fingers. Earlier, before I spilled the bubbles, June had called me into the kitchen. She was gazing into a pan of rice left over from supper. "You've got to try this—touch this rice, feel the texture. Squeeze it! This is so far out!" The hash her boyfriend Will had left us was excellent that night.

But June's not here. Joel isn't here. I run out the door; it slams behind me. It's almost dark outside. I rush back up the street. There must be somebody I know among the crowds of people clutching rocks and swerving from one block to another. Tear gas spreads like a poisonous cloud, making it harder and harder to breathe. I thread my way between people milling about on Embarcadero del Mar. I don't know any of them. Two guys smash an empty patrol car with sledgehammers—boom! Boom! Metal on metal. Pure delight bubbles out of me in a happy laugh. I jump up and down and punch my fists in the air. Yes! Justice for that poor black dude they beat up after the Kunstler speech! I walk down Pardall to the other side of the loop, searching until I spot Velvet and her boyfriend Cyril in the middle of the crowd on Embarcadero del Norte. She and I were dorm mates our first year at University, and this quarter she's in my existentialism class. I push my way through the crowd and walk up to them. Cyril looks horrible, frightening. His lips curl in a snarl and expose gritted teeth. His jaw is clenched like a fist. His black plastic glasses are all fogged up, and blood oozes from his nose. He doesn't have the camera he usually brings everywhere. "Wow! What happened to you?" I ask. "Did you get hit by a rock?"

"No." His voice is stuffed up and muffled. "My nose started bleeding the minute they shot off that fucking tear gas."

It's dark, and the round streetlights look like glowing balloons floating in the hazy gas cloud.

"I'm trying to get him to come home," Velvet swipes a lock of black hair out of her face. Her mouth trembles and she looks about ready to cry, and not from the tear gas.

"No fucking way—I'm not missing any of this shit!" Cyril says. There's blood all over his face and soaking his sleeve. He swipes his arm across his nose, which makes it bleed even more. Some of the blood gets on his glasses.

"Look," I say. "You won't miss anything." I spread my hands, gesture toward the crowd. "This'll be going on for hours. You can just get some ice on that nose, get the bleeding stopped, and come back. Bring a wet towel to put over your face the next time they gas us—and bring your camera. Document all the shit going down."

"Yes—you can come back!" Velvet agrees. "Come ON!" She yanks his arm, but he's a big man and she can't budge him. Then with a loud pop, a tear gas grenade lands six feet away, and everybody runs. The three of us run up Picasso Street toward the apartment building on the edge of campus where Velvet and Cyril live.

At Velvet's apartment, Cyril heads for the shower. I wander around the living room and study the black and white photos tacked up on the walls: Velvet sitting, close-ups with just her face, a majestic oak tree, dogs, and photos of the beach. Cyril is a student at Brooks Institute of Photography in Santa Barbara.

Velvet sinks into a brown, tweedy upholstered chair underneath the oak tree photo and twists her locks of curly black hair every which way. "This is so horrible."

"I know. It's a really bad scene." I plop myself down on a kitchen chair. The dining area is at the end of the living room farthest from the door. Three studies of a bunch of carrots decorate the wall here.

"Let's have some wine." Velvet pushes out of the chair, goes to the refrigerator, and takes out the Red Mountain vin rose. She unscrews the cap, takes a long swallow, and hands me the jug. I take a big gulp of the sour, watery brew. She pulls up a chair next to me and we pass it back and forth. The wine starts to taste better after the first few mouth-puckering sips.

"You know," Velvet says, "I'm not a bit sorry about Isla Vista Realty. They didn't give me back my deposit last year and I cleaned that place spotless! I broke one of their windows myself." She sinks back into her chair and takes a moody sip.

"So, are we celebrating then?" I stretch out my legs and rest my feet on the red vinyl seat of one the other chairs.

Velvet passes me the jug. "No way—this whole thing is so freaky, how it escalated into a complete war zone. And Cyril is acting crazy—that's what scares the shit out of me!"

Sudden raps on the door make us jump to our feet. I dash across the living room carpet to the coffee table, grab the bag of marijuana, and shove it under a couch cushion. Velvet sidles over to the door and puts her eye to the peephole, tensed up like she's ready to run for her life. Then she relaxes. The breath she'd been holding whooshes out and she pulls the door open. David, who lives across the street, steps inside. With his pointed elfin face, long red-gold hair and green eyes, he looks more like a rock star than the math wizard he is. David has an unfortunate fondness for purple clothes, which are very hip but clash with his hair and freckled skin.

"Hey, man—you've got to come see this. They're looting the Bank of America!"

We stare at him. "No way!" I offer him the jug of Red Mountain.

Cyril comes out of the bathroom, a towel around his waist, giving his head a vigorous rubbing with another towel. "What's going on, man?"

David prances back and forth like a kindergartner about to wet his pants. "Get some clothes on already—they're looting the bank! Come ON!"

It's much quieter outside than it had been. The police are gone, but clouds of lingering tear gas hang in the air. The street lamps are dim in the smoggy haze.

"What happened to the police?" I say.

"Couple of cars fuckin' got destroyed." David grins at me. "Freaked the pigs out bigtime. Then every time they started advancing on us, this time we didn't run. We came right back at them, throwing rocks. They're used to being the ones doing all the terrorizing, beating the shit out of people and they just couldn't handle it. They fuckin' *fled!*"

Velvet and I look at each other. I know her uneasiness mirrors my own. It'll be only a matter of time before the cops come back. Maybe they'll be in helicopters and mow us all down with machine guns… but the destruction of that patrol car was a wonderful thing to see.

Cyril snaps photos. "Not enough light," he complains. "Gonna be blurry as hell without a tripod." But he goes on taking pictures anyway.

All the lights are on in the bank. The broken doors stand open and the fluorescent glare spills out onto the sidewalk. Overturned furniture and loose papers cover the floor along with broken glass, pens, rubber stamps, and smashed adding machines. A crowd has gathered; everyone stands and stares at the ruined bank. Slowly, we all form into a silent line, and we file through the bank and out again. No one says a word, and nobody touches anything; we're paranoid about fingerprints and being caught later with anything from inside that bank. I worry about the surveillance cameras. Are they filming our procession through the rubble under the harsh, white lights? But for some reason I don't understand, it feels important to be here, as if we are somehow documenting what has happened. I think we all sense that this is a turning point, that our lives will never be the same.

"Do you want to come stay with us?" Velvet asks when we're back out on the sidewalk. We step into the shadows, out of the light pouring from the bank. She gives me a worried look. "I don't think it's safe here."

I shake my head. "Thanks, but I need to get home in case Joel calls."

"Ahhh." The corners of her mouth turn up just a bit in a sympathetic, rueful smile. "That's right. He flunked out, didn't he?"

I throw up my hands. "Yeah. I alternate between pining for him and wanting to kill him." I shrug. "Anyway—see you in class tomorrow."

At the same time, Velvet, Cyril, and I all step towards each other. We all come together in a three-way hug. We stand on the gritty concrete and press against each other as tight as we can, then break apart, arms still touching, reaching out as we separate.

"Call me when you get home," Velvet says. "Let me know you made it."

I thread my way through the crowd; elbows jostle me before I come to the edge of the sidewalk and step into the street. David is next to a dumpster talking to a couple of cute girls in mini skirts, one dark-haired, one blonde. I have to laugh; both girls are cow-eyed and I wonder which one he'll take home tonight. I head back home through the dark streets. If Joel were here, we'd nudge each other, roll our eyes. We'd laugh at those girls and joke about which one would get lucky. Friday night, he'll jump in his Bug and race up the freeway. He'll be here by 1 a.m.—how many hours until I see him again? Way too many... But this has gone beyond just waiting. Today was a total blowmind—William Kunstler's magnificent speech in the stadium, the riots afterward, the police, the tear gas, the procession through the ruined bank—it was all so important and he wasn't here for any of it. We're not sharing our lives anymore. It feels as if a cold wind is scouring out my insides. If the apartment is still empty when I get home, I don't know what I'll do. But from half a block away, I see light in the windows, and I run the rest of the way.

I yank the door open, then stop short, my hand on the door jamb. June is on the couch with *Essentials of Paleontology* on her lap, her baggy gray UCSB T-shirt not quite covering a pair of red plaid men's boxer shorts, one bare foot propped on the coffee table, the other curled underneath her. It could be just another ordinary night. The Band is playing on the little record player on the side table, "Up On Cripple Creek." [2]

"How can you study at a time like this?" I ask. Doesn't she *know?*

She sticks her yellow highlighter into the center space between the pages and sighs. "I'm not seeing a word. At this rate, I'm going to flunk this course for sure." She closes the thick black textbook over the highlighter, lays it on the coffee table, and slides her bare feet into a pair of Birkenstocks waiting on the rug.

I sink into the couch next to her. My left hand moves up to my hair all by itself without my being aware of it. My fingers select a long strand and twist it up tight. "Did you see the bank?" I tug on the twisted lock of hair.

"Yeah, I walked past it—fuckin scary! I just wanted to get home. Rioting's not my thing…" She runs her hands over her short auburn hair, smoothing it. "I had to come back anyway; Will's coming."

Will is the other LA boyfriend, only he's older, a balding bartender in his 30s who looks like William Shakespeare. His name is an eerie coincidence, and I wonder if he secretly writes sonnets and plays as a side job when he's not bartending. Will always brings a supply of premium quality dope, the kind that would enable someone to write things like *The Tempest* or *Midsummer Night's Dream*.

I push back my hair, heave myself up from the squishy couch and pad into the kitchen. I pick up the phone and dial Velvet's number. Nobody answers; I'll bet Cyril is still out there taking more dark, blurry photos. I take a pint of Carnation chocolate ice cream out of the freezer and rummage through the silverware and utensil drawer until I find two spoons. I bring it all back to the couch and hand one of the spoons to June. We dig in.

"Thanks," June says. "This is just what I needed."

"Comfort food," I agree. We pass the ice cream back and forth and spoon up cold, creamy mouthfuls until we've hit the bottom of the carton.

Outside, a car pulls into the driveway. The door swings open and Will steps inside, Shakespeare in a gray cotton sport shirt and spotless Levis. He gives June a quick kiss on the lips and then looks up. "Something's burning," he says. "Let's go find out what it is."

The night sky has turned a smoky orange color. The three of us hurry up the street as people come out of their apartments to stare at the huge column of flame lighting up the sky. It casts a weird glow. It must be a couple of hundred feet high, blazing up into the night. It's the Bank of America.

We circle around to the front of the bank, where the intense heat has shattered the windows of Borsodi's coffeehouse across the street. Downed power lines like giant rattlesnakes sizzle on the pavement. The dying trees surrounding the bank make me want to cry, but at the same time, the tower of flame fills me with wonder—the sheer power of it blazing up as high as I can see, metal girders and cables white hot and melting in the inferno—it's an awesome sight.

"It's terrible," says Will after a while, "and yet, so beautiful."

I'm itching to call Joel, but it's hours past midnight. I can't call his parent's house in the middle of the night! I'll have to wait until morning to tell him about the bank.

I phone him before I go to my morning classes. I'm still in the baggy navy blue T-shirt I use for a nightgown, the same one I had on when he showed up unannounced for our first date.

"Wow—you won't believe the heavy shit going on here," I say. "There was a serious riot yesterday—people started smashing windows, cop car got torched—"

"Gnarly!" he exclaims. I've never been to his house, but I picture him padding up and down the hall in his bare feet, the long phone cord stretching out behind him.

"It was like police and tear gas all over the place until the pigs gave up," I say. "They actually left when they couldn't subdue the people." While we talk, I pace back and forth between the kitchen sink and the avocado green fridge.

"Oh fuck! Shit! I wish I could've been there!" His frustration explodes and I hear a crash over the line as he kicks the wall and something falls over and breaks.

I grip the phone tighter. I feel his powerless fury all the way across miles of phone lines. It's so totally wrong for us to be separated. "Man, I really, really wish you were here too," I say. "That was just the beginning. I don't know who did it, but somebody broke into the Bank of America, looted it, busted stuff up, and then later they set fire to the whole thing. Burned it to the ground. You should have seen the fire! I've never seen anything like it in my life! It was awesome!"

"Fuck! All the time I was there, the place was just dead, like a cemetery. Then as soon as they kick me out, stuff starts happening… Fuck. I'll be there tomorrow night, soon's I get off work."

"Isn't there any way you can take a day off? Come tonight instead?" I hear the words come out of my mouth before I know what I'm saying.

He lets out his breath in a long sigh. "No, Darlin', things are getting heavy down here too. Draft board is already breathing down my neck—fuckin' University must have let them know the minute they kicked me out. Remember that draft lottery back in December?"

"Yeah, but I didn't worry too much because you were in school." I fiddle with the phone cord.

"I got number 67. That means I'll get drafted for sure. My folks hired a hotshot lawyer to fight it, hopefully get me off. I don't dare do anything to piss them off right now."

"Oh, Nooooo!" I suck in my breath. My legs get shaky and I sink to the edge of one of the kitchen chairs.

"It'll be okay, you'll see. I can always go to Canada if it comes to that. Just hang on; I'll be there tomorrow night."

"Okay. I love you."

"Love you too, Darlin'."

I pry the receiver out of my sweaty hand and set it back in the cradle. My stomach clenches into an icy ball. No way will some lawyer be able to get the Army to reject a surfer athlete like Joel! I hadn't been that worried; I imagined there would be so much bureaucratic red tape, the draft board wouldn't even notice until he was back in school again. I forgot that red tape slowness only happens when people need help from the government, not when the government wants something.

My first class is in ten minutes—no time to figure out what I'm going to wear. I pull on yesterday's jeans. The T-shirt I slept in will have to do. I slip my bare feet into my worn black Buckle Skitter Capezios.

There's no time for a leisurely walk to school; I'll have to ride my bike. I unlock the rusty blue Sears three-speed chained to the metal handrail next to the porch steps and stuff my books into the wicker basket in front. I hop on, coast down the driveway, and pedal up Sabado Tarde Road past apartment buildings and duplexes. The white plastic bicycle seat digs into my butt. I hate that seat; I avoid riding my bike as much as I can.

There's a nasty, smoky smell in the air that gets stronger as I come to the ruins of the bank. I stop, put my feet on the ground, and stare. The bank is an ugly, still-smoldering jumble of twisted metal and rubble from collapsed walls. It looks like it was hit by a bomb. The smell of burnt plastic and charred office equipment and electrical wires makes me cover my nose with my hand, but it doesn't help. People in medieval times carried oranges studded with cloves for this kind of thing. Across the street, the heat-shattered shop windows are boarded up. Someone has come during the night and fixed the downed power lines. I hoist myself back on my bicycle seat and race towards school.

I have a full day of classes. Afterward, I go to the library to study. I take the elevator to the eighth floor and find a quiet spot at one of the shiny wooden worktables. I'm reading *Twelfth Night* for my Shakespeare class, but the mistaken-identity plot is silly and the mean-spirited pranks don't make me laugh. My mind wanders so much it takes ages to get through the play, and I stare at the long rows of tall metal stacks without seeing them. What if Joel has to leave the country? Canada doesn't like our war and provides asylum to people fleeing the draft. They'll let him in for sure. But what about me? I doubt if their open door extends to girlfriends. I hope that lawyer can find some way to keep him out of the Army, but I can't imagine how.

It's way past suppertime when I come to the end of *Twelfth Night*. I push my chair back and get up. I stretch my hands up toward the ceiling and lean left, then right. I wiggle my butt to get the circulation back and shove the wooden chair with its hard seat back against the table. I gather my textbooks and notes and carry them to the elevator. I push the "down" button and wait. It comes. The silent metal doors slide open like portals on a spaceship and I step inside. I hit the round button that says "1" and the elevator descends. Elevators make me dizzy, as if I'd left part of myself on the top floor, and the enclosed space gives me a sick feeling. What if it gets stuck partway down? The elevator reaches the ground floor and the doors slide open. My legs feel wobbly; I'm glad to step out onto solid red tiles. I go outside and down the concrete steps to my bicycle. I pedal to the UCen (University Center). There are vending machines in the cafeteria where I buy an apple and a packet of powdered sugar mini-donuts. I get watery instant coffee from another machine and sit down by the dark window to eat my supper. The tart juiciness of the apple complements the powdery donuts and I wolf them down. A couple of older men in tweed jackets, probably profs, smoke and drink coffee several tables away. They're the only other people here. The huge room is lonely and creepy, a sea of empty tables. Metal girders crisscross the high ceilings. The dark windows along one wall reflect the emptiness and make the cavernous space look vast. It seems to go on forever. I need to go home. I throw the apple core, half-drunk coffee, and donut wrapper in the green metal trashcan on my way out to the bike rack.

I pedal past the art department and head toward Pardall Road, but at the campus edge, a line of police cars blocks the way into Isla Vista. I stop, slide off my seat and straddle the bike. Two cops in helmets swing their clubs and smack them against their gloved hands as they swagger up to me.

"Just turn that bike around and go right back," the shorter one tells me. "Nobody gets past this point." He sweeps his baton toward the path leading to campus as if he's directing traffic.

I freeze. I can't move. I don't even breathe.

"Go on," the cop barks. "Back the way you came."

"I... I—But I need to go home!" My throat closes up on the first words, then the last part tumbles out in a rush: "I live on Sabado Tarde."

"Yeah, right!" the short cop sneers. He smiles, but it's a mean smile, a shark's grin. He steps closer and I shrink back. My left pant leg catches on the bike pedal and I almost fall down.

"What're you doing out so late?" the taller cop demands, his feet planted a good distance apart for stability. He shifts his hands on the club, grips it hard like he's about to hit me.

"I've been at the library, studying." The words come out high and squeaky. I reach into my basket to pull out my Shakespeare book, to show them—

"Hands out where we can see them!" barks the tall cop, and I freeze. The other cop comes over with a flashlight and paws through my books with gloved hands.

The two cops look at each other and shake their heads. "No weapons, just books," the shorter one says. He sounds disappointed.

"Ohhh kay—" The taller cop drags out the word and then pauses.

Minutes drag by. I stand still, hands clenched on the handlebars. The shorter cop shifts his club from one hand to the other and back again. The cops look at each other and shrug.

"Weeeelll, I suppose you can give it a try," the taller cop says at last. "Go all the way down to El Nido and make your way back from there. Stay away from the center of town." He waves me on with his club.

El Nido Lane is at the end of the road, near the beach. I get back on my bike and pedal past more police cars. Fear clutches my body like a giant icy hand and it's hard to move. My legs shake as I pedal. I try not to wobble—if I swerve, they might think I'm going for a sudden attack. I imagine cops hiding behind the eucalyptus trees with guns trained on me. But why are they here? Why have they blocked the streets?

I reach the end of the road. I turn onto El Nido and steer down the narrow street past oak trees and rows of apartment buildings. I hear yelling and what sounds like firecrackers. When I get to El Embarcadero, where there's a clear view, I stop. At the bottom of the business loop a couple of blocks away, police cars line the street and crowds of people surge back and forth in a cloud of tear gas. What the—? I just want to get as far away as I can. I turn and go the opposite direction toward the beach, then onto Del Playa, the street where Joel used to live, and make my way home from there. Out here, it's quiet and peaceful. A breeze from the ocean tangles my hair. It smells like salt. Maybe it will blow away the tear gas.

June and Will have already gone to bed, but they left a lamp on for me. The living room looks cozy in the yellow lamplight. It feels safe here. I lock the door, set my books on the coffee table, and shrug the tension from my shoulders. I can't wait to crawl under the covers. June comes out of the other bedroom. Her hair is rumpled and she looks like a sleepy 12-year-old in her sleeveless white cotton nightgown with eyelet around the neck and armholes.

"Kate—Thank God you're back! Where were you? We were so worried."

"I was at the library," I say. "Why? What happened?"

"There was a rally," June says. "Apparently things deteriorated." I follow her into the kitchen. She flips the light switch and the sudden brightness makes us both squint. The teakettle sits on the stove, the burner on low. Steam drifts out of the spout. June opens the green-and-white Seelect herbal tea package waiting on the counter and shakes reddish-brown chunks of sassafras root into a teapot. She pours in boiling water and shuts off the burner. I get mugs out of the cupboard, spoons from their drawer, and milk from the fridge. We bring everything to the table.

June switches off the light. "Ah, much better." She picks up a book of matches and lights a candle that sits on the table next to the honey jar.

I jump up, close the curtains, and come back to my chair. The kitchen feels safe now. "Cops hassled me on the way home," I tell her. "They didn't want to let me into IV at all, but they let me go after they rummaged through my stuff. Guess they figured out I was harmless. It looked like there was another riot from what I could see a few blocks away."

June pours tea into our mugs and we stir in honey and milk. She nods. "Somebody lit a bonfire after the rally, and all of a sudden there were helicopters flying around, ordering everybody off the streets. Will and I were coming home from Santa Barbara—we went out for Chinese food—and we made it back before the police came."

The tea tastes like root beer. I'm glad June had the hot water waiting; sassafras tea is so comforting. "This really hits the spot," I say. I wrap my hands around the warm cup. "So what happened next?"

"Well, we didn't see any of it, but I was getting worried so I called Velvet to see if you were at her place. Obviously you weren't, but she said the police came in with their clubs and tear gas and it was just like yesterday before the bank burning. People didn't leave. They fought back."

"It's still going on," I say.

"Oh, that's just great." She gets up and puts her mug in the sink. "I hope we're far enough away so it doesn't keep us awake all night."

"Me too."

6

GIANT WATERBUGS

In the Red Lion Bookstore, "Helter Skelter"[1] from the Beatles' White Album plays on the stereo. The Red Lion always has wonderful music. I dance past tables with rare, expensive books on display to the poetry section against the back wall. I want to find the poem by William Butler Yeats that says "Things fall apart, the center cannot hold." I peer at the rows of books. Wilde, Wordsworth, Yeats—Yes! Here it is. I pull the red paperback off the shelf, then sit on the floor and leaf through it until I find the poem, "The Second Coming." I cross my legs, lean back against the bookshelf, and read.

> "Turning and turning in the widening gyre
> The falcon cannot hear the falconer;
> Things fall apart; the center cannot hold;
> Mere anarchy is loosed upon the world…"[2]

This is the one. I lumber to my feet. The bottoms of my jeans have come out of my black leather boot tops and I bend down and stuff them back in. I carry the Yeats book to the counter. The clerk, his brown hair pulled back in a ponytail, is reading Heinlein's *Stranger in a Strange Land*. The frames of his thick black glasses have slid down his nose and he pushes them back up. I fish a five-dollar bill out of my pocket and lay it on the counter with the Yeats book. He gives me change and slips the book into a paper bag. He slides it across the counter and goes back to Heinlein.

"Thanks," I say. I'm about to leave when I see Velvet's shaggy black mohair sweater over by the table with the big art books. She knitted that sweater herself, bit by bit, the year we were roommates. I'd know it anywhere. I take the paper bag with my new book and cross the dark red carpet to find her leafing through a volume of Salvador Dali's paintings. Velvet has been coming back again and again since the book first appeared on the table. It's an oversized, very expensive edition; no one can afford to buy it.

I peer over her shoulder. The page is turned to "The Persistence of Memory" with its melting clocks. "That bank burning was as surreal as anything in the Dali Book," I say.

Velvet runs her fingertips lightly over the page. "I wonder what he would think if he were here." She turns toward me and lifts her hand to her cheek. Her eyes are dreamy and unfocused.

I shrug. "I'll bet he'd love it. Life is so ordinary most of the time. If he'd been here that night, he wouldn't have needed to distort it with his imagination."

Velvet closes the Dali book, giving it a long, yearning glance as if it were a lover, or chocolate, before she turns away. We amble to the door of the bookstore, past the display rack with Rod McKuen's poetry books, embarrassing wallows in cheesy sentimentality. The books have brilliant hued, glossy covers—*Listen to the Warm, Stanyon Street, Lonesome Cities...* All best sellers. *"Listen to the Warm"* is lettered in purple and magenta over bright orange and yellow splotches; it reminds me of the equally cheesy "Light My Fire" poster in all the guys' apartments.

Velvet jabs my bag with her index finger. "What have you got there? Is it *Listen to the Warm?*" She grins, eyes full of mischief. The Beatles have moved on to "Savoy Truffle;" they're singing about sweet, sticky desserts.

"Yeah, right! No, it's Yeats," I laugh and stuff the bag into the big pocket on the inside of my gray-green fatigue jacket that I got at the army surplus store for fifty cents.

"Ah. No gooey Pablum for Kate." She shakes her head and purses her lips like a finicky baby.

"I do like the more meaty stuff," I agree as I pull the door open, but a throbbing roar, so loud it's like a blow, swallows my words and drowns out the Beatles. "What the hell?" I yell, but I can't even hear my own voice.

Three helicopters circle overhead like gargantuan waterbugs. It's cloudy, and the dull-gray sky makes them even more menacing. The propeller blades make an ear-splitting whap-whap-whap sound, and a distorted, mechanized voice repeats the same message over and over again. "The governor of the State of California has declared a State of Extreme Emergency. Effective immediately, a 6 p.m. to 6 a.m. curfew will be strictly enforced. All roads will be closed. No one will be allowed in or out." I cross my arms over my chest, army jacket hugged tight around me. What in the world? 6 p.m.? What time is it now? I'm not wearing my watch. All I know is that it's late afternoon.

Oh no—This is Friday! Joel is coming tonight!

Velvet has her hands over her ears, eyes wide. Her short purple corduroy skirt flaps around her black tights as we run back inside the Red Lion. "Helicopters are outside! Big, hideous ones!" Velvet waves her arms in a circle, like a propeller. All the customers jerk their heads up and the clerk stands behind the counter with his mouth hanging open.

Everyone freezes for a couple of seconds, then they all surge toward the door like stampeding buffalo, including the clerk. Velvet and I jump out of their way. The door swings open and lets in a blast of helicopter din and distorted words before it closes.

I lean my back against the wall to the left of the door and slide down until I sit on the floor, legs out in front of me. The Beatles have come to the last song on the album, "Good night, sleep tight." Their soft voices are like a caress. I slump forward. A sudden scratchiness rises up in my throat and I swallow hard. Oh, to be tucked safe into bed... But I have to leave. Velvet is over by the window, peering out. I get to my feet. My army jacket has slipped and I shrug my shoulders back into it.

"I gotta split," I say. "Have to tell Joel he can't come tonight. I was counting the days—what a fucking drag!" I grab the door handle.

"Just be careful," Velvet says.

The roar of the helicopters throbs in my bones. I hold my hands tight over my ears, but that doesn't help; even the ground vibrates. My fast walk turns into a run. I sprint like a rabbit fleeing a wildfire, my own heartbeat pounding in time with the underground throbbing. My breath comes in gasps as I push for more speed. The whole world is coming apart, just like in the Yeats poem! I'm halfway down Sabado Tarde Street when the choppers wheel in unison and head back toward Santa Barbara.

In my own place, I sit on the edge of my bed, yank off my boots, and shrug out of my jacket. It slides off the bed onto the floor. I'd better wait and catch my breath before I call Joel's house. He won't be home; I'll be talking to his parents. I need to be careful. I have to sound like a calm, responsible person, not some hysterical nut case. The last thing I want is for them to start ragging on him about me. I've never met them but I know they must have a low opinion of me. They probably think it's my fault he flunked out. I lean down, pull the paper bag out of my jacket pocket, and take out my new book. I stretch out on the blue India print bedspread and turn on my side. I leaf through the poems, but the words swim on the pages in meaningless patterns; no way can I concentrate right now. I'd better get that call over with. I swing my legs to the floor and sit up. I pick up the army jacket and hang it over the back of the wooden desk chair. See? I'm a responsible person.

I pad into the kitchen, get a glass from the cupboard, and fill it from the sink faucet. I sip while I eye the phone on the counter. The water is cool on my throat and I gulp the rest; I'm thirsty after running all the way home. I set the glass in the sink. Okay. I take a deep breath and dial Joel's number.

His mom picks up the phone. "Oh, he's not home," she says when I ask for Joel. I picture Joel's mom to be an older, dried-up version of him in a cashmere sweater and pearls. Regal. Not motherly at all.

I twist the cord around my finger. "Could you please give him a message at work?" I imagine her swatting the air with her free hand, wishing she could swat me out of her son's life.

But her voice is warm. Friendly. "Of course." Now I don't know what to picture.

I sink down into a chair. "Thanks," I say. "Please tell him to call me before he leaves."

"I will. And you be careful!" she warns me. "The governor was on TV. He called the UCSB students cowardly little bums and was talking about martial law. What a schmuck—he's calling in the National Guard!"

"What? Really? Oh, no!" I cross my legs and tug on the phone cord. Martial law? I stare at the window. The sun is setting; soon it will be dark outside. I don't see any troops out there.

"You take care now," Joel's mom says. "Just lay low. Call us if you need any help."

"Uh... Everything's pretty quiet right now. But thanks so much." I stare at the phone receiver after she clicks off. What the fuck? After a moment, I get up and place the receiver back in its cradle. I wipe my sweaty forehead with my sleeve.

The door bursts open and June drags her bicycle into the living room. She has a grim look on her face. "Did you hear? We're going to be on lock-down at 6. It's like Attica or something." She pushes the bike over the dingy carpet into her bedroom and leans it against the wall.

"Yeah—those choppers going 'Extreme emergency' were like something in a war movie—it felt like we were in Vietnam." I sit on the couch and cross my arms. I hug myself tight—just thinking about the helicopters gives me a cold feeling.

The first military jeeps arrive a little after 6. They cruise up and down the streets with bullhorns. "Clear the streets! This area is under Curfew!" June and I peek out from behind the kitchen window curtains as the jeeps barrel down Sabado Tarde. A sheriff's pickup truck with what looks like a machine gun mounted in the back speeds by. There's a loud pop and a cloud of tear gas billows up on our front lawn. Black-and-white patrol cars, black California Highway Patrol vehicles, and the National Guard all cruise past our house. More pops shatter the air; it's impossible to tell where they're coming from.

I move away from the glass and walk toward the living room. "We'd better stay away from the windows. What if some of those shots are bullets?"

June peers out one last time before she lets go of the curtain and turns away. "You're right," she says. "They've gone crazy out there. It'd be just like them to glimpse movement and shoot us."

The burning, peppery smell of tear gas seeps in underneath the door and I run to the bathroom, my hand over my nose and mouth. I turn the water on, dampen washcloths to hold over our faces and grab a towel. I bring it all into the living room, hand a washcloth to

June, and wad up the towel in front of the door to keep any more tear gas from coming in. Why hasn't Joel called?

June frowns at the door. "Probably won't do much good. This crummy building is full of cracks." She coughs into her washcloth.

We sit beside each other on the floor, backs against the wall next to the kitchen.

The phone rings and I jump up and grab it off the counter, then sit back down. But it's Will, and I hand the phone to June. I blink back tears. I press the wet cloth to my eyes. This is waiting for that phone call ratcheted up a hundredfold. What if he didn't get the message? What if he drives all the way here only to find the road blocked?

June takes the receiver. "Oh Baby," she says. "You're not gonna believe what's happening—police are on the rampage! You are so damned *lucky* you had to go back to LA this morning!" She clenches her free hand into a fist and pounds the floor three times. "This is a nightmare!" she wails.

Oh God, is she going to tie up the phone now? All of a sudden I hate her. Sure enough, she's going on about the helicopters and the curfew and the tear gas and the National Guard and—but now she says, "I've got to go, Sweetie. We're trying to get hold of Joel so he doesn't come and get himself arrested or worse. I'll call you back."

Tears overflow and spill down my cheeks. My nose is runny and all stuffed up. I gulp in my breath as June hangs up and relief washes over me. "Thank you!" The words come out in a honking sob.

June holds out her arms and we hug there on the floor as I gulp and sniff. "It'll be okay, I know it will," she says. "His mom isn't going to forget about something like this."

I let go of her and nod. I use my washcloth to wipe my nose and eyes. It feels cool on my hot face. I take a hiccupy breath. "I know."

The phone is on the floor where we can both reach it. We sit on the carpet, backs against the wall, legs stretched out in front. Outside in the dark, vehicles keep driving past our duplex. I strain my ears, listening to the deep rumble of the jeep engines, waiting for the phone to ring. I tell myself he'll call when five more cars go by. I count them: One, two, three, four… five! But the phone remains silent. I lift the receiver to make sure it is connected. The dial tone sounds in my ear. I hang up the phone and wait.

After a while we get our books and try to read our assignments. I go over the same paragraph about Albert Camus again and again, but I don't retain a single word.

Joel doesn't call until after ten. "What's up, Katie Cat?"

"Oh, thank God you got my message! You can't come tonight. They've closed the whole town off. Blocked the roads." I sit cross-legged on the carpet and hunch over the phone while I tell him about the curfew and how many police and soldiers are patrolling the streets.

Joel just laughs. "Like hell is that going to stop *me*!" I imagine him at the other end of the line in some dreary office with plastic bins full of mail needing to be sorted. He'll be in one of those swivel chairs with his feet propped on the table. There's a slurping sound and I hear him swallow. I'll bet he has a bottle of Hansen's natural apple juice. He doesn't drink sodas.

I touch my hair, separate a strand out, and tug on it. "But they'll catch you for sure," I say.

I look sideways at June. She just grins and gives me a thumbs-up. "He'll make it."

"No, really," Joel says. I hear the glass bottle thonk down on the desk. "It'll be fine. I'll just park on the campus and sneak in on foot. This is gonna be fun. Leave the light on for me—or, come to think of it, don't do that. I'll come tap on your window and you can let me in."

No way can I sleep. I snuggle under the blankets, close my eyes, and try to relax. In freshman psychology class, the instructor brought in some weirdo to teach us about hypnosis. It didn't work with me; I just stared at the idiot swinging his pendulum back and forth ("You are getting very drowsy now"), but before the hypnotizing part, there was a relaxation session. I use that technique now. "Concentrate on relaxing the muscles of your scalp... now move down to your forehead. Let all the frown creases relax, go smooth..." It's no use. Behind my eyelids, my imagination plays out horrible scenes—Joel stopped by the police, dragged out of his car and arrested, Joel trying to ram the car through a roadblock and the police opening fire the way they did in *Bonnie and Clyde,* Joel being beaten...

The soft drumbeat of fingers on glass comes sooner than I expect; he must have pushed that Bug hard. I throw off the covers, slip out of bed, and go to the window. There he is, grinning at me in the dark. He gives me a thumbs up, then waves toward the front of the building and I run to let him in. I kick the towel out of the way and yank the door open the minute I hear his boots on the concrete steps. I pull him inside and then his arms are around me. He crushes me against him. I bury my face in his shoulder and breathe in his scent of soap and Herbal Essence shampoo. Relief floods my whole body like cool water and I squeeze him tight. I wrap my right leg around his left one. I work one hand into his hair, short now but still shaggy, and we kiss. He tastes like apples.

I lean my head on his shoulder. "I can't believe you got here," I breathe into his ear. "I'm so glad you made it."

He takes my face in his hands and kisses the tip of my nose. "All the pigs in the State of California couldn't stop me!" The corners of his mouth turn up in a lazy, cat-like smile. His eyes are bloodshot; he must be so tired. "Oh, I almost forgot," he says. "I promised to call my folks when I got here and let them know I'm safe." The smile disappears and he sighs. His hands drop to his sides; his shoulders droop.

"Yeah." I touch his elbow. "Go ahead. Your mom was really cool when I called—blew my mind. I think maybe the reality of the war is expanding her consciousness."

"Hunhh—" His breath comes out in a snort. "Really? For me, it just feels like major sucking up I have to do to pay them for getting that draft monkey off my back." His lips press together and turn downward. He runs his hand through his hair and shuffles into the kitchen.

"I'll be in the bedroom," I say. The rotary dial makes a string of fast clicks like the metal beads on a keychain as I pad into my room. The red Yeats paperback is still on the bedspread and I set it on the windowsill. I'll bet Joel would like these poems; I'll tell him about Yeats in the morning when we eat breakfast. Outside the window, little water droplets glisten on the arbor vitae hedge. It has started to rain.

Joel is laughing when he steps into the bedroom. "They want to meet you," he says. He closes the door.

"Huh?" I spin around and stare at him. "That's a surprise." But I don't want to talk about Joel's parents now. I'm naked under my flimsy cotton nightgown and I pull it over my head with one swift motion. I fling myself onto the bed. "C'mere," I say.

His face lights up in a big grin. It only takes a few seconds for him to peel off his own clothes while I watch. He flips the light switch and darkness envelops the room. It's a lush darkness that feels primeval and I squirm on the bed, waiting. Then he's on top of me. "Now this is the kind of welcome I like," he growls, and kisses my shoulders, my breasts, my belly button, and I moan. I wrap my arms around him and pull him in, all the way.

We settle into the rhythm of it now, slow at first, then building to a slamfucking crescendo. Afterwards we lie sprawled together, slippery with sweat, my head on his chest, his arm curled around my back. "It was easy sneaking past those pigs." His voice is sleepy. "No problem at all."

"I love you," I say, but he's already asleep.

7

SHADES OF PLAID

Joel and I are in the back seat of his dad's old green Plymouth Valiant. It's Saturday evening, and we're stoned. At the time, it seemed like a good idea to smoke a doobie before having dinner with Joel's parents, it would maximize our enjoyment of the wonderful restaurant we're going to. Now, I run my fingers over the nubbly, cream-colored seat cover crisscrossed with brown and orange stripes that almost look plaid, but not quite. An image of Hamlet on stage pops into my mind. He's decked out in the same fabric and the skull in his hand wears a perky fake plaid beret. What would Hamlet say? "To be plaid or not to be—" which has me in helpless giggles.

Joel sprawls against the car door, legs stretched out, his boots all the way across the bump in the middle of the floor. "What?" he asks.

I purse my lips and try to look serious. "To be plaid, or not to be," I intone in a solemn voice while I stroke the seat. "Methinks thou art but a poor seeming of plaid—"

"A plaid woven by an idiot—signifying nothing," Joel finishes.

I try to hold in my giggles, to "maintain," but the hilarity escapes in a loud snort. Joel pretends to punch my arm before laughter bursts out of him too.

A deep chuckle rumbles out of his dad, Aaron, who is driving. Aaron doesn't know about the joint we just shared on the back patio. He thinks he's laughing along with us, in on the joke. Aaron looks sharp in a black fedora and gray cable knit wool sweater. The backs of his hands on the steering wheel have a lush growth of black hairs.

May, Joel's mom, sits in the passenger seat. She's about as far as you could get from the ice queen I pictured when Joel talked about her. She's tiny. Her short brown hair with red highlights and blue harlequin glasses give her a perky look. She turns and smiles at us.

Jefferson Airplane plays on the car radio. Grace Slick sings about "Lather,"[1] a thirty-year-old child in an adult's body.

This is surreal! Do they really listen to this kind of music? My parents' car radio is always locked on the station that plays "Back to the Bible Broadcast," out of Lincoln, Nebraska.

This is a celebration. The draft lawyer got some doctor to state that Joel's feet are so malformed and flat that he can barely hobble short distances, let alone march. Joel has been declared 4-F, unfit for military service. He sits next to me in a clean blue work shirt tucked into a new pair of jeans that stretch tight over his strong thighs. He looks perfect, and so healthy I still can't believe they found a way to make him 4-F.

Aaron and May had to take out another mortgage on their home. They're drowning in debt now, but they didn't hesitate; for them it's well worth it. They'd do anything to keep Joel from going to Vietnam.

I had expected his parents to be rich, but they live in an ordinary tract house in one of those neighborhoods built all at once with three different house plans, so the homes are pretty much identical. Joel told me the kids growing up there knew exactly where all the rooms were in other people's houses; it just depended on which of the three plans they had.

Aaron drives an old 1960 Valiant with almost 100,000 miles on it.

But their boy is safe. The news came last Wednesday when he was at work, but he couldn't wait to tell me the news. "I'm free!" There was so much joy and relief in his voice that I imagined him jumping up and down on the desk and doing cartwheels in that dismal office that I've never seen. "No draft! No Army! No Vietnam! I don't have to run to Canada!"

"Yes!" I yelled. I drummed my own feet on the floor and punched my fist in the air. Afterwards I danced around the living room. Now we're going out for a feast. Joel chose the Aware Inn on Sunset Boulevard.

Every weekend, he makes that drive up to my place. He hasn't missed a single Friday since he moved back in with his parents. He doesn't have to sneak in now; little by little, life in Isla Vista has returned to normal. The National Guard withdrew at the end of the weekend after the bank burning, and the bank reopened in a temporary trailer module. This afternoon, Joel took me back to LA with him to meet his parents.

It's like a family outing. Joel and I ride in the back seat like a couple of little kids. It's getting dark and stripes of light and shadow from the streetlights and neon signs flicker over our faces. Joel looks like a tiger peeking out from behind a clump of tall grass.

"You know, Kate," he says under his breath so his parents won't hear, "You really remind me of a Siamese cat."

I want to purr. "Meow!"

May turns around. Her eyeglass lenses flash silver. "What did you say?"

"Uh…" Joel nudges my foot, and I giggle. "We were talking about this cat that keeps hanging around my apartment," I say off the top of my head. "It drives me nuts going meow-meow-meow until I feed it."

Joel's eyes gleam in the dim light, His hand creeps across the seat like a cat stalking a bird and pounces on my knee. "Gotcha," he whispers.

My fingers are a split second away from landing on his hand when it jumps off my knee and skitters up the back of the seat. Our hands chase each other like a pair of kittens, or spiders. I'm so stoned that our fingers look like shadowy spider legs.

"Joel tells me your dad was in the Merchant Marine," Aaron says.

We put our hands back in our laps. We face forward. I yank my skirt down to cover my thighs. We need to maintain.

"That's right," I say. "Dad was in the Merchant Marine during the war. His ship almost got torpedoed. They saw it coming underwater—it just barely missed."

"That's scary!" Aaron says. We stop at a red light, and May and Aaron both turn and stare at me.

"That's what *he* said." I twist my fingers together and wiggle my toes inside my best brown lace-up boots that look like something Amelia Earhart would wear.

"I was in the Merchant Marine just like your dad," Aaron says. "I was in charge of radio communications—monitored all the messages coming in from everywhere."

"Oh... short wave radio?" Everything is happening in slow motion now. I hope my voice doesn't sound as dragged-out to him as it does to me.

"Right. I still have a ham radio set. Sometimes I stay up all night talking to people all over the world."

"Far out! When there's a ship on the horizon, my dad takes a spotlight down to the beach. He'll, uh... flash it. You know, talk to them in Morse code—find out where they're from and where they're going."

"That's a terrific idea! I'm going to try that!" Aaron turns to face the windshield and bangs his hand on the steering wheel for emphasis. The light changes, and we continue on down a wide boulevard with six lanes.

May turns to smile at me over the top of her seat. "You're going to like where we're going. Lots of stars eat there—Eric Clapton, Warren Beattie, and once I saw Paul Newman!"

I smile back. "Did you see *Bonnie and Clyde?* Warren Beattie was really good in that."

"Yes, I cried when they got killed," May says.

"Me too."

The Aware Inn is a natural foods restaurant on the "Sunset Strip." It's all heavy beams and natural wood. Hanging plants and climbing vines are everywhere; it's like being in a forest glade. We sit around a heavy wooden table. Joel is on my left, Aaron on my right. May sits across from me. I unfold the linen napkin and spread it on my lap over my suede miniskirt. All of a sudden, there's a gnawing hole where my stomach should be, and it's growling. It feels like I haven't eaten for days. I pick up the tall menu with entries in elegant script. The vegetables are all organically grown. The beef is organic and grass fed. The chicken is free range. I don't care—I want to throw the menu down and say, "Just bring me two of everything!"

"This place is really good," Joel tells me. "This is hands-down my absolute favorite place to eat. Anything you order will be good."

"I think I'll have the steak with wild mushrooms and veggies," I say.

"Yeah, I'll probably have that too. I'm starving," he says.

A long-haired waiter who looks like Mick Jagger seems to appear out of nowhere. With a flourish like a circus ringmaster, he sets a basket of hot whole-grain rolls in the middle of the table along with a giant mound of butter on a plate. The sudden aroma of bread just out of the oven makes me feel faint. I have to put my hands under my thighs on the seat of my chair so I won't grab one of the rolls and wolf the whole thing down before anyone else even starts. Joel doesn't care. He has already broken a roll in half. He slathers it with butter. He's the reason we're celebrating. Right at the last minute, he's been snatched out of the grinding jaws of Nixon's war machine. He can do no wrong tonight.

I sip my water with a slice of lemon in the glass. When I look up, Aaron is talking to the waiter about wine. I wait until May has a roll before I take one. I don't feel stoned anymore, just ravenous. Oh, why did I do this? I always forget about this part of smoking dope, the part where the high wears off and blood sugar plummets so low that it's agony to have to think about good table manners.

Mick Jagger the waiter comes back with a bottle of merlot. He turns our upside-down wine goblets right side up. He pours a little in Aaron's glass. Aaron swirls it around, takes a sip, and nods. Now Mick circles the table and pours wine for all of us.

I butter my roll, sink my teeth into the hot, yeasty bread, and tear off a chunk at last. Mmmmm, wonderful! I want to cram the whole roll into my mouth but force myself to slow down and take bites. I pick up my glass and taste the wine. I'm used to the kind that comes in a jug with a screw-on lid; all that stuff people say about body and bouquet is lost on me. It's good though.

Mick is back, and we order. Besides our entrees, Joel requests something called the "Aware Salad."

After Mick goes away, Aaron clears his throat. We all look at him, and he raises his glass. "A toast!" he cries. "To end the war!"

We reach across the table and clink our glasses together. "To end the war!" we all say, and take big swallows of wine.

May sets down her empty goblet and looks around. She picks up her water glass and takes a sip. "I don't recognize anyone tonight," she says. "How about you, Kate? Any rock singers?"

I hold up my finger and chew up the chunk of bread I just stuffed into my mouth while I glance around. I don't see anybody I know. I wash the bite down with the last of my wine.

"No," I say, "I don't see anyone, but our waiter looks just like Mick Jagger of the Rolling Stones. It can't be, but he does look like him." I don't tell her I've been secretly calling him Mick in my own thoughts.

Joel nudges my foot with his boot. "Don't you be getting the hots for him," he jokes.

I nudge him back. "Naw, he's not my type. No plaid." The stoned feeling comes back for a minute and we glance at each other, then look away quickly, our months twisting into contortions as we hold in our laughter.

Mick brings four plates and a huge wooden bowl heaped with romaine lettuce, grated beets and carrots, sprouts, avocado, cucumber, sunflower seeds, and pine nuts, all tossed together in a lemony herb dressing.

May gives him a sly look as he begins to dish out the salad. "What's your name?" she asks.

"Rudolph Aquarian, Ma'am."

May and I look at each other. We both shrug at the same time.

I would never have dreamed of grating raw beets into a salad. So many different flavors—boring iceberg lettuce with sliced tomato and thousand island dressing will never taste good to me again! I'm full of plans for my next trip to the grocery store. I try to work out what's in the dressing—lemon, mustard, oregano… it's tangy, so good. Joel wolfs down his salad and loads up his plate again. I'm going to figure this out—learn how to make this or something like it. He'll be so surprised when he comes to see me next weekend!

When our steaks come, I don't find much that I can duplicate. The succulent beef isn't the same as what they sell in the supermarket.

"What kind of mushrooms are these?" I ask Joel. They're as meaty in their own way as the beef.

"I have no idea, but they sure taste good!" He bumps my left knee with his right one under the table and we grin at each other.

"How's your chicken, May?" Aaron asks. She has a stuffed chicken breast in a thick sauce.

Her mouth is full and it's a moment before she can answer; she nods fiercely as she chews. "Heavenly!" she says.

Aaron is eating something flat and white with a honeycomb texture mixed up with butter beans and hunks of sausage. I try not to stare but it looks so weird.

I set down my fork. "What *is* that?"

"Tripe," he cuts off a chunk and forks it into his mouth. "It's a delicacy. Want to try some?"

"No thank you," I say.

"Believe me, you're really missing out. Most Americans have such a limited definition of food." Aaron stabs another lacy-looking piece and swabs it around on the plate to get lots of gravy, or juice, or whatever it's swimming in. He lifts the fork to his lips and pops the morsel into his mouth. "Mmmmm."

I turn to Joel. "Is it really good?" I ask him.

"I don't know and I don't intend to find out." His lips curl in a moue of distaste.

I look at May, raise my eyebrows.

She shakes her head. "You have to develop a taste for it," she says.

Oncoming headlights stream by like schools of strange fish in a black ocean. The Bug's lights illuminate just a small stretch of road ahead with the yellow line on the left. White metal upright road markers flicker past on my right. Inside the Bug, the backlit speedometer hovers around 70. The numbers on the radio dial glow green; the little red tuning indicator is at 1110. "When I was young"[2] is playing. I can't get enough of Eric Burdon's deep, growly voice.

I pull my maroon fake fur coat around me and snuggle into its warmth. "Your folks seem really nice," I say.

"Yeah, I can see where you'd think that." Joel stares straight ahead at the road, hands lazy on the bottom rim of the steering wheel. "But what you saw is just the surface."

"Oh..." My hand creeps up to my hair as I digest this. I pull on a lock and twist it. "You mean they really don't like me?"

"They probably like you fine. For sure they like that you're graduating. But that isn't what I meant—I was talking about me. Their insatiable need to control everything I do."

"Oh, wow." I stare at him; he's still looking at the road, but now his hands grip the wheel tight. "I never thought of it that way. I was just blown away that they hate Nixon and the war—they seem so *enlightened* compared to my parents. But yeah—they could still be heavy control freaks."

"You can say that again. And they've really got the screws in now that they saved my sorry ass from Vietnam." Joel presses the accelerator and the Bug leaps forward.

I let go of my hair and fold my hands in my lap. I sit up straighter. "Have they planned your whole life out for you like my parents have for me?" According to my folks' plan, I'm supposed to move back home right after I graduate. Mother has a job lined up for me in the same medical office where she works... *exactly* the same thing that happened to Joel!

"You bet your ass," Joel says. "Only I don't *want* to spend my life as a fucked pincock in some straight office job." He slams his hand on the wheel. "So they want me to see a psychiatrist to get to the root of my lack of motivation."

I clap my hands over my mouth, but laughter explodes against my palms in a blast like a fart.

"What?" He stares at me, eyes narrowed for a couple of seconds before he looks back at the road.

"They fix you up with a pure drudgery job and then send you to a shrink to find out why you don't like it." The absurdity of it makes me dissolve in helpless giggles. "All in the nicest possible way, of course," I manage when I can speak again.

Joel bursts out laughing along with me. He takes his right hand off the steering wheel and squeezes my knee. "Oh, Katie, I don't know what I'd do without you."

His words warm my insides all the way down. We're meant to be together, and we both know it. "That goes both ways," I say. I lean across the center console and run my fingers down the side of his face.

8

INNOCENCE

"Do you ever wish you were still little?" June asks. She and I sit cross-legged on the avocado shag living room carpet in Barbara's next-door apartment, eyes locked on the black-and-white TV on a metal stand. The news is on.

I pick at the fuzz on my new 501 shrink-to-fit jeans. It takes a few washings before the raw denim gets smooth. "No," I say.

Five feet away, three-year-old Alicia lines up her family of stuffed animals—Winnie the Pooh, a gray-and-white stuffed cat with brilliant green eyes, a sock monkey, a fluffy blonde cocker spaniel, and a brown-and-white Steiff horse with a red leather bridle. When I was nine, I wanted that same Steiff horse more than anything else in the world besides a real horse. Alicia is so lucky.

Barbara teaches third grade. She knocked on our door an hour ago and asked us to come over and stay with Alicia while she rushed back to the school to pick up the work for tomorrow's lesson plan. She'd somehow arrived home without it.

On the TV, Governor Reagan, his face twisted with rage, outlines his policy for dealing with student demonstrators: "Appeasement is not the answer. If it's to be a bloodbath, let it be now." I feel cold inside. His words and the hatred on his face scare me—he's just like Daddy raging about the Communists.

"When I was little," I tell June, "my dad got that same ugly look sometimes. He talked like that too. He wanted to put Joan Baez in front of a firing squad because she started the Institute for the Study of Nonviolence."

June stares at me, lips parted, eyes wide. "No shit! Was he crazy?"

"Maybe. The idea of nonviolence totally freaked him out." I lean back on my hands and stretch my legs out in front of me. My left foot has fallen asleep and I wiggle it. Pins and needles shoot through my toes. "He went to John Birch Society meetings, and you'd have to be insane to do that."

"Or ignorant." June rolls up on her knees and flips the TV dial to Porky Pig before she sits down again.

"He never finished high school," I say.

"What I meant about wanting to be a kid was *her*." June nods toward Alicia in her blue corduroy shorts and a red, blue, and green striped T-shirt. Her tiny bare feet are dirty and her long brown hair is tangled. "It would be so nice to be like that, with no worries…"

"Yeah," I agree. "I wouldn't mind being her at all. And how far out to grow up in Isla Vista!"

Porky Pig wears a jacket and bow tie but no pants. His piggy tail sits on the middle of his butt like a nasty little rosette. He dashes back and forth across the screen in time to Prokofiev's *Peter and the Wolf*. He talks in a high-pitched, manic stutter that makes my insides clench up. I can't stand that pig. I can just see him behind the wheel of a patrol car. I reach for the power switch but happy giggles make me drop my hand back in my lap. Alicia's watching, her stuffed toys forgotten. Delight makes her brown eyes shine.

The door swings open and Barbara sweeps into the room, one arm wrapped around a fat blue cloth-covered binder.

"Mommy!" Alicia jumps to her feet. "Did you bring me anything?"

Barbara reaches into the pocket of her car coat and takes out a Milky Way.

"Oh goody!" Alicia takes the candy bar over to her stuffed animals and sits down. Her eyes focus on the television as if she had never looked away.

"What do you say when somebody gives you something?" Barbara's voice is sharp.

"Oh. Thank you, Mommy." Alicia tears open the wrapper and takes a big bite as she watches the little pig.

"Thanks, guys," Barbara sighs. She sinks down on the orange and brown tweed sofa. "Everything go okay?"

"Yeah," I say. "Alicia was perfect—totally entertained herself so we could watch the news... which *wasn't* okay. Reagan's not going to stand for any more student demonstrations." I lumber to my feet and test my weight on the foot that fell asleep. Pins and needles are almost gone.

June gets up and slips her feet into her Birkenstocks. She glances at Alicia, who's laughing at Porky on the TV screen, before she speaks. "He said there would be a bloodbath," she tells Barbara, her voice lowered. "He actually said that."

Barbara motions us to come close and we walk over and lean down to listen. "I'll bet that son of a bitch had a hard-on while he was saying it," she whispers.

The UCen study lounge is empty except for me. I nestle into one of the gray easy chairs with an abstract flower design in splotches of darker gray and faded blue, my books piled on the blond wood end table beside me. I curl my legs to the side and tuck my feet against the arm of the chair. There's a hole in my black tights from when I fell off my bike and scraped my knee.

The room is so quiet. Everyone has gone to a rally; Nancy Rubin is here instead of her husband, Jerry, who was scheduled to speak today. He's a political activist and one of the Chicago 8. Chancellor Vernon Cheadle cancelled the speech and banned Jerry Rubin from coming to UCSB. Anger hangs over the campus. It's dank and stagnant and seeps into every corner like thick fog, making everything feel wrong and off kilter. Cheadle's action violates the First Amendment, freedom of speech, and people are shocked and outraged. But what else should we expect from the same guy who fired anthropology professor Bill Allen? After Reagan's bloodbath speech, I feel like nothing will surprise me ever again. Just remembering those helicopters and the whole town in lockdown gives me the chills. I can't stop thinking of the way those trucks barreled down the street shooting off tear gas—if Reagan has his way, next time it will be bullets along with the tear gas.

I ought to go hear Nancy Rubin, but I have too much work to do before the weekend. Having Joel show up every Friday gives me a lot less study time. Somehow, I talked my way into a graduate seminar on the Brontes. Professor Swann let me in because there was still room after all the graduate students who wanted to had signed up. My paper for his class is about the religious influences in the Brontes' work, but what fascinates me most is the lives of the Bronte children and the fantasy worlds of Glass Town, Angria, and Gondal that they created. They wrote book after book in tiny script that was too small to be read by adults. I sigh and pick up *Jane Eyre*. What can I say about the infamous Mr. Brocklehurst, who starved the children at his school so he could hoard the money for himself? His excuse was that by starving their bodies, he was nourishing their immortal souls—how did he get away with it? My own parents and their church cronies are fundamentalist evangelical Christians; I've had to listen to their sanctimonious twaddle all my life. It disgusts me so much I can't be objective. I glare at the pale gray wall, the empty chairs, and the big round table in the center of the room. To write a dispassionate essay on this very hot topic will be good for me.

I scribble a few notes. The whole culture was riddled with destructive beliefs so people like Mr. Brocklehurst could take advantage, just like that pious warmonger, Billy Graham—things have not changed that much. My stomach clenches. I've got heartburn; a sour, scalding burp erupts in my throat. I'm not getting anything done here; I should have gone to that rally.

I pedal up Pardall road on my way home from the UCen. It's getting dark. I turn left on Embarcadero del Mar. The pavement is wet. Puddles are everywhere, as if there has been a big storm. David sits on the curb in front of the Isla Vista Market, bare feet in the water, faded purple pants rolled up to his knees. I brake and hop off my bike.

"Where did all this water come from?"

"Some idiot opened the fire hydrant," he says. "The market got flooded before they got it shut off."

"No shit! What happened?" I hoist the bike up onto the sidewalk.

"People are really pissed off." He lifts one foot out of the water and examines his muddy toes. "Were you at the rally?" he asks.

"No, I was hitting the books. I'm getting behind so I decided to pass on Nancy." I scrape the sole of my shoe on the wet cement. "Did I miss anything?"

"Well, Nancy was in a snit because they wouldn't let Jerry come. She was talking about revolution, and she brought some other guy with her that was going 'Kill the pigs!'" He looks up at me; intense green eyes bore into mine. "It kind of tied into how everybody's feeling right now." He sloshes his foot back and forth in the water.

"Yeah," I agree. "We're all pissed off, for sure."

"I think the bank's going to burn again," David tells me.

"I'll go check it out," I say. "See you around." I get back on my bike and pedal around the loop to the temporary bank structure. A crowd mills around in the parking lot. Some jocks stand in front of the bank, guarding it.

Rocks crash against the bank trailer and a jangling alarm shatters the evening quiet. It goes on and on and I want to put my hands over my ears. The crowd surges up to the bank but the jocks hold firm.

"Come on," one of them yells. "Be cool! The last thing we want is to bring the pigs in to occupy this town again."

That's for sure. I turn my bike toward home. I make the turn onto Sabado Tarde and pedal fast to build up speed.

June sprawls on the purple pillows piled in a living room corner. She looks like a soldier in her army surplus camouflage pants and olive-green shirt. She has a bottle of bubble soap and a plastic wand. She purses her lips and blows a little at a time until an enormous bubble quivers on the wand. Rainbow colors flow and swirl in psychedelic patterns on the bubble's transparent surface. Bob Dylan's "Blonde on Blonde"[1] album is playing. I throw myself on the couch, put my feet up on the coffee table and lean back with my hands behind my head. The lamplight is warm and yellow and I go limp as tension flows out of my body. June blows bubbles in my direction. They float through the air for a few seconds, then wink out.

I heave myself up from the squishy sofa, walk over to June, pick up a pillow and sit down on it. "Let me blow some."

She passes over the red plastic bottle. I blow a stream of little bubbles and watch them pop, one by one. I give her the bottle and work my fingers into the hole in the left knee of my tights. "It's heating up out there," I say. "Looks like that trailer the bank is in might get burned down."

"Oh, shit—I knew it!" June picks up a pillow and throws it across the room. It bounces off the couch and lands on the floor. "But you know what I think? Cheadle can't be so stupid that he didn't know canceling Jerry Rubin would cause a reaction, especially with everybody so upset about Bill Allen. He's probably taking his orders from above. They *want* us to riot so they can make an example of us." She screws the top back on the bubbles and sets the bottle on the table next to the lamp.

"Whoa! That's a horrible thought." I feel cold all of a sudden. I smooth out the cotton skirt that I made from a piece of an India print bedspread. I try to make it cover the hole on my knee but it's way too short.

"Yeah. Hell yeah. What the fuck are we supposed to do?" June heaves herself up out of the pillow corner and stomps over to the coffee table. She picks up a green spiral notebook with UCSB in big blocky letters on the cover.

"Probably the only thing we can do is get through this semester, graduate, and leave this insanity…" I get up too, put my pillow back on the pile, and come back across the room on my way to the kitchen.

"I made some rice," June says, "if you haven't eaten."

"Thanks! I just came straight back from studying—I'm starved."

It's still quiet when we go to bed after a couple more hours bent over our textbooks.

I fall asleep, and the next thing I know, I'm in a dream where I'm on the beach a couple of miles up the coast from Isla Vista where an oil well pump like a giant dinosaur swings up and down. It groans as it pumps. A cable attached to its head chains it to the well. Its sad creaks and moans are full of despair. It will never escape. I'm not supposed to be here, but I can't stop watching. I wish I could help.

A thunderous voice bellows out over the groans of the oil well, something about "Extreme Emergency." The pump stops and five policemen with rifles now stand on the metal beam that looks like the dinosaur's back. Five gun barrels are pointed straight at me. Shots ring out, and I disappear into a black void, falling, falling…

I'm back in my bed. My heart slams against the inside of my chest like it wants to escape and my baggy T-shirt and underwear are soaked with sweat. All of it still feels real. I sit up in bed, stare at my familiar dark room with its wooden dresser, desk, clothes piled on the chair, and listen. The rumble of a truck engine fades into the distance.

I get up, pad into the bathroom, and pee. Back in my bedroom, I strip naked and take a clean shirt out of the middle dresser drawer. I pull it on over my head. Fresh underwear comes out of the top drawer. The truck sounds louder now; it's coming back. I run to the kitchen and peer out the window. Here it comes—it's a big dump truck with three bullhorns on top of the cab, pointing forward and to both sides.

"This is a state of extreme emergency!" a faceless voice in the bullhorn squeals, Porky Pig with no stutter. "Clear the streets! Clear the streets! A curfew from 6:30 p.m. to 6 a.m. is now in effect and will be strictly enforced." Cops ride in the truck bed, protected by the high wooden sides. They point what look like shotguns at the houses and apartments as the truck passes by. There's a loud pop and a tear gas canister explodes on the lawn next door to our duplex. I pull up a kitchen chair and sit down. I rest my elbows on the windowsill and gaze out as another truck rolls by with more gun-wielding cops. I squint and stare hard, but in the dark, I can't tell whether these are rifles or shotguns. The sheer menace of it gives me an icy feeling in my chest that spreads into my stomach and arms and constricts my throat. But this can't be real—police don't ride around in dump trucks. I must be still dreaming.

"Holy shit!" June says behind me. "Nothing like getting jolted out of a sound sleep. I have a test in the morning."

"At first," I tell her, "I fitted it into the dream I was having. I dreamed they killed me—that woke me up!"

"Whoa—that is so heavy." June slides another chair next to mine and joins me at the window. It's not long before another big truck barrels past, this one going about 35 miles an hour.

I get up and go out to the living room. There's a radio on the top bookshelf and I switch it on. It's tuned to KCSB, the campus radio station. "Isla Vista has been sealed off," the announcer says. "California Highway Patrolmen have blocked every entrance into IV to both vehicular and foot traffic. A curfew has been declared; no one is allowed on any public street between 6:30 p.m. and 6 a.m. and during the day, people are not allowed to loiter or gather in groups of more than three persons."

Hearing it on the radio somehow makes it more real.

A sad, heavy feeling settles into my chest and belly instead of the icy fear. What in the world has happened? This used to be a safe, sleepy town. I was never afraid to ride my bike home from the University library after it closed, and I'd walk the streets by myself in the middle of the night to clear my head after a marathon study session. In between classes and all-night cram sessions, there'd be parties and street dances. It seemed like there was always a band playing somewhere.

Why do they hate us so much?

We grew up in constant terror that at any moment, bombs could obliterate life on this planet. Somewhere between the air raid drills in grade school, war in Vietnam, racism, and the assassinations of JFK, Martin Luther King, and Bobby Kennedy, we got lost. Now we're searching for a new road home. The civil rights movement and anti-war protests are beacons on that road. The explosion of new music, the funky clothes, and the psychedelic art bring us together and make us feel like change is possible. Full of hope, we gather in our crummy apartments with bookcases made of cinder blocks and boards and talk about new ways to live. We play the Beatles, Jimi Hendrix, Ritchie Havens, and Donovan on our cheap little record players while incense burns. The joint we pass back and forth becomes something holy. And outside are uniformed, Gestapo-like police in cars and trucks, on foot, and in helicopters overhead who are extremely threatened by us and want to eradicate us off the face of the earth.

We're just kids, but somehow we have committed an unpardonable sin.

9

PLAYING IN THE APOCALYPSE

The police said he was killed by a sniper's bullet. They said Isla Vista was full of snipers with high-powered rifles. They lied. They knew that same night that Kevin Moran had been shot by a police officer, but they stuck to their sniper story for three full days.

Friday morning, I flip through the hangers in my closet and take out my green mini dress with navy blue smocking around the neck. I pull it on over my pink, orange and purple flower-print bra and underwear and tug it down. I rummage through the pile of shoes on the floor of the closet until I find my left sandal wedged underneath one of my boots. The right one is in the corner behind all the other shoes. Long leather thongs hang from a hook and I take them down. I pull the straps out of the front and side parts of my sandals and thread thongs through instead. I slip the sandals on my feet and crisscross the thongs up my legs, knot them tight above my knees. The headband I made hangs on the same hook, and I take it down and jam it on my head. I braided it with four thongs the same way we made plastic lanyards at summer camp. It has a long tail that hangs all the way down my back. Four turquoise blue ceramic beads dangle from the strands at the end. It's thick and heavy and will make dents on my forehead. I am the only person in Isla Vista with a headband like this and leather thongs lacing up my legs. I feel strong and powerful when I wear them. I need that boost right now; I feel shaky and have a sick feeling in my stomach. I check the full-length mirror on the closet door. I look confident and brave.

I step outside and go down the stairs. Who knows what I'll find downtown? There might not even *be* a downtown—God knows what happened to bring in the police dump trucks with their guns and tear gas in the middle of the night.

It's a sunny day. Wispy cloud tendrils float far above. An airplane crosses the sky underneath them.

I walk fast down Sabado Tarde and am halfway down the block when a salty breeze comes in from the ocean. I breathe it in—there is no smell of burning. I hurry around the loop at the bottom of Embarcadero. In the Bank of America parking lot, the oblong office trailer still stands. I thought there would be a smoking pile of rubble, but other than a few rocks scattered on the asphalt, you'd never know anything happened here. The fraternity jocks must have held off the people who wanted to burn the bank... so why did the cops take over and seal off the whole town? What was with those huge dump trucks? And the curfew? The trucks are gone now; the invasion in the middle of the night doesn't seem real. Did I dream that, too?

A black patrol car with a white roof cruises by and slows down to a crawl while the two cops give me the old lookover. Their lips open in toothy, predatory grins and I freeze. Just for a second, their eyes bore into me as if they have x-ray vision to check me out underneath my dress. I feel like Little Red Riding Hood. *Ohhh what big eyes you have... The better to see you with, my dear.* The cops laugh. The driver guns the motor and they peel off down Embarcadero toward the beach.

I cross the street to Borsodi's Coffeehouse. It's how I imagined the beat hangouts in San Francisco when I was about fifteen. I so wanted to be a beatnik. I dressed in black, took up the guitar before I discovered I had no musical talent, and wrote angry poems about my parents like the one that said "Mother. She calls herself my mother." Inside the door at Borsodi's a hand-lettered sign reads: "There should be common ground somewhere, after all, where free spirits can gather and not seem peculiar and out of the way." [1]

It's dim inside, with small, black tables and wooden chairs. There's a stage at the back with a piano. The walls are a collage of folk art, pictures of clowns, psychedelic posters, street signs, quotations, and postcards. There's a shelf crammed with old hardcover books that look like library discards. A chess set in the middle of a game sits on one of the tables; the players left without finishing. I sit at a table near the back. The owner ambles over. He's a dark-haired, thirtyish man in a woven green and black Mexican poncho. "Very cool sandals! What would you like?"

"I'll have a Viennese coffee," I say. "What happened last night?"

"Well…" He shifts his weight from one foot to the other and back again. He plants his hands on his hips. "There was a back-and-forth thing going on; lots of talking. Some people wanted to torch the bank; some were arguing against it. Know what I mean?"

"Yeah, I passed that scene on my way home around supper time." Elbow on the table, I lean my face on my hand and look up at him.

His eyebrows lower and a crease forms above his nose. "I doubt anything would have come of it besides a broken window or two. It was getting late. There weren't even that many people, but all of a sudden out of nowhere the police came charging up in these big trucks—must have been going about 50 miles an hour. Mayhem! There was so much tear gas you couldn't see anything. Everybody ran." He brings his hands together, spreads his arms out wide. "They chased people up the streets, firing shotguns—it was mostly girls they shot. It was criminal."

"Whoa, that's heavy!" I run my finger over the uneven surface of the table. It's a collage of clown faces cut from old magazines, glued down and lacquered over with a yellowish glaze. I always try to get this table. "We got woken up in the middle of the night when they drove by with their bull horns going 'Extreme Emergency,'" I say.

"The thing is," Bob Borsodi leans in like he's telling me a secret. "Nothing was really going to happen to that bank this time. It would have fizzled out. They created that extreme emergency all by themselves and now we've got a police state again. I'll bet that bank *will* get torched now. You want a bagel with that Viennese?"

"Yeah, that sounds really good. Thanks."

I take the phone off the kitchen counter and sit cross-legged on the linoleum floor, my back against the cupboards. I take off my headband and put it on the floor next to me; the weight of it has given me a headache. I shake my head, whip my hair around, and massage my scalp with my fingers.

I pick up the phone and dial Joel's number. I hope I've timed this so I catch him between surfing and the time he has to leave for work.

"Hullo?" The sound of his voice makes me grin in spite of the reason I'm calling.

"Hi," I say. I don't know where the phone is in their house, but I picture him in the kitchen, just like me, only standing.

"What's up?" he says.

"Bad news," The receiver is in my left hand, and with my right, I pick at the knot that holds up the thongs that crisscross my left leg. It's always a bitch to get these things untied. "We're on lockdown again."

"Oh, fuck! What happened? Bank burn down?" Rapid footsteps tell me he's pacing the floor now.

"No. The bank is fine. I really don't know what happened. There was sort of a demonstration, but…" I work the knot loose and unwind the thong; it has left indentations all the way up my leg. "I was at Borsodi's and Bob said the pigs just came in these big trucks with no warning and declared a state of extreme emergency so they could seal off the town—June and I were asleep and the trucks woke us up." My eyes feel prickly and I swallow hard. I tug at the other knot on my right leg. "Bob said they shot girls with their shotguns. I'm scared."

"It's okay." His voice is reassuring. "Don't worry. I'll be there as soon as I can."

"I don't know, Joel. It's worse this time. They're in these big old dump trucks like tanks. High sides, police with guns pointing over the top." The knot blurs in a haze of tears, but I feel it come loose. I gulp. I haven't committed any crime, but it makes no difference—they'll kill whoever they feel like killing. Those girls they chased with their shotguns hadn't done anything either. This isn't about securing the peace. This is about making an example out of us, to make people afraid. "Did you ever hear of police in dump trucks?"

"Uh, no…" I hear the refrigerator open. I was right; he's in the kitchen. There's clink of glass on tile, then a gurgling sound; he's pouring himself something to drink. "Look," he says. "I know a lot of ways into IV. I'll do my best to get in, but if I can't, I'll check into a motel and call you from there."

"You're my hero," I tell him.

A deep chuckle ripples out of him and I can see the grin on his face just as if he were here. "Yeah? Really?"

"Absolutely," The way he eats up compliments makes me smile. "But be careful. I need you in my bed, not on some bug-infested cot in the jail."

"Okay, Darlin'," he manages between bursts of laughter. "Keep that bed warm. I'll see you tonight!"

I hang up the phone, take my sandals and headband into the bedroom and throw them back in the closet. I slither out of my mini dress. After the way the pigs leered at me, I just want to blend into the scenery, be invisible. The pair of jeans I wore yesterday hangs over the back of my chair and I pull them on and button the fly. I yank open a drawer, take out a gray UCSB T-shirt, and tug it on over my head. I'm almost late for my first class. I grab my books and run to the door barefoot, unlock my bicycle and pedal fast. "Hey Jude"[2] plays in my head. It's about making things better. That's what I want my life to be about. I want to make things better, but mostly I just struggle to get by. At least I try not to make it worse.

June and I are in the back yard of Sun and Earth Natural Foods. We sit at an old, weather-beaten wood table under a tree with bowls of sticky short-grain brown rice mixed with Tamari sauce, vegetables, and cheese. Sunflower seeds are sprinkled on top. We gulp cups of hot Mu tea, a sweet, rich brew of 16 different herbs. Indian sitar music drifts out from inside the store. Six-thirty, curfew time, comes and goes, but instead of leaving, we slow down. We finish every last bean sprout, sprig of broccoli, and grain of rice. We look at each other without speaking. Electric bulbs hang from the trees and light up the place like a fairy garden. We take our dishes down the shredded bark path to the serving counter and put them in the plastic tub waiting there.

"What say we just have a look around before we head on home?" June says. "It drives me nuts to sit at home and not know what's going on."

"Just a second..." I bend down and stick my finger between my sandal and the bottom of my foot where a piece of bark has slipped in. I shake my foot. Mother would say if I picked my feet up when I walked instead of shuffling, this wouldn't happen. The chunk of bark falls out and I straighten up. "Yeah, lets go see what's happening. Is Will coming tonight?"

"Nah, he's waiting until tomorrow. Joel?" June leans her elbow on the counter.

"He's going to try. Idiot." I try not to grin.

She claps her hand on my shoulder. "You know you love it."

We take the path out of Sun and Earth's back yard. We're just half a block away from where the street curves in a loop that connects Embarcadero del Norte with Embarcardero del Mar. Hundreds of people mill around the loop area. June and I mingle in with the crowd like fish entering a stream. We stop and listen to snatches of conversation around us...

"I say let's burn that motherfucker!"

"Ambulance came, took Pamela to the hospital. They picked more than fifty pellets of shot out of her back..."

"Where are the cops? It's after curfew, and they're not here..."

"Burning the bank a second time is pointless, man. It'll just give them an excuse to justify all the brutality..."

June and I thread our way between people. Elbows jostle us and the background roar of the crowd turns into angry shouts as people argue about what to do. We cross the street to the Magic Lantern Theatre and sit on the low brick wall that borders the roofed walkway. From here, we can see what's going on without being swept up by the mob.

In spite of the curfew, there are no police. Do they intend to rush in all of a sudden the way they did last night? My muscles are tensed, ready to bolt. The absence of police feels ominous, I know it's deliberate and whatever they've planned won't be good. Will we be able to escape into the dark and make our way home? I gaze at the crowd; people meander up and down the block. It's getting cold, and I pull my army jacket closed, button it, and cross my arms. "I don't want to be here when the police come," I tell June.

"No kidding," she agrees. "And they'll come, no question about that." She swings her feet back and kicks the wall. "What do you think about burning that crappy bank trailer?"

"I don't care one way or the other," I say. "I think the police will come and terrorize the town no matter what happens—what we do or don't do won't change a thing."

A couple of guys drag a garbage can into the street, pour something in, set it afire, and melt back into the shadows. The fire only burns for a couple of minutes before a dude wearing a fraternity sweater comes with a fire extinguisher and douses the flames.

"You are totally right," June says. "How silly—as if putting that fire out is going to make any difference. Macho jock do-gooders!"

We leave when somebody pushes an old car out into the street and sets it on fire. I hate to see the car burn; I hate waste. I'd love to have that car—any car. But I can't afford one.

Back at the apartment, we sit on the sofa. The radio is on, tuned to KCSB 91.5. Their reporter watches the bank area from Borsodi's across the street. He coughs so much he can hardly speak as he tells how six police trucks barreled in, crashed through a barricade people had built to block the street, and surrounded the bank. The tear gas is so thick it has leaked into the coffeehouse, and no one can see what's going on outside. But someone shouts the news that there has been a shooting. An ambulance comes and takes the victim away.

The first truck rumbles by outside our duplex. We hear shots, and I'm afraid for Joel. I hope he has checked into a motel in Santa Barbara, far away from all this...

But the door flies open. Joel stumbles in his rush to get in, yellow surfboard under his arm, eyes wild. "Where's the butcher knife?" he yells. "They shot my car—I barely made it! No way are they taking me alive!" He drops the board on the living room floor; it thuds on the carpet as he runs to the kitchen. I trail behind him. He jerks open kitchen drawers, one after another, with a great clatter of silverware and utensils. "God DAMN IT! Where is it?" I pull the butcher knife out of its wooden block on the counter and hand it to him.

I step to the window and peer out at the street. "Where *is* your car?"

"Down the block. I left it next to some apartments and hid in the bushes. I don't think they saw me come here, but I'm not sure." He stands with his feet planted apart, butcher knife in his clenched hand. It's a cheap knife, dull from years of chopping meat and veggies and sawing crusty bread loaves. His face is clenched too, determined. His eyes dart around as if he expects cops to materialize out of the walls.

June locks the door. I help her drag the couch in front of it. We sit on the floor, our backs against the sofa, and wait while Joel stands next to the kitchen window and peeks out from behind the drapes. He leans forward and studies the street outside, tense and alert. The trucks keep lumbering by, but they don't stop in front of our duplex.

"Joel," I call out. "Come tell us what happened!"

He peers out the window one last time, then ambles into the living room and sits on the floor next to me, jean-clad legs stretched out. He uses his feet to pry off his tennis shoes. His arm slips around my shoulders and he plants a quick kiss on my cheek. "Told ya I know all the ways into the town. Drove without lights, pulled into dark spots and ducked down until the trucks went by. They were shooting everything in sight. They shot out all the street lights and I heard a bullet go whangggg somewhere on the back of the car…" His arm flies out sideways.

"Oh, shit!" I say.

June just stares at him. Her mouth hangs open.

"You know," he says, "now I've had a chance to think, I'll bet it was a random bullet. They probably didn't even know I was there."

The reporter on the radio says the only people left in the downtown area now are police.

June stands up. "I'm going to turn in. I'm wasted after no sleep last night." She puts her hand over her mouth to cover a huge yawn.

Joel and I get up too. We hold hands and lean together. We bump against each other as we go into my bedroom. I close the door. We don't bother to turn on the light. He takes off his jeans jacket and pulls his shirt off over his head as I wiggle out of my Levi's. We don't hang up our clothes or fold them. They fall to the floor in a pile and we step on them. Naked, we ease onto the bed. We hold each other, press our bodies together as tight as we can, skin to skin, and we stay that way for the longest time.

"Somebody at the bank got shot tonight," I tell him. "I am so glad you made it here safe!"

"You think it was a random bullet?" he asks.

"No," I whisper.

"Shit!" He lifts himself up on one elbow and leans his head on his hand. He looks down at me. Anguish flickers across his face. "What if this is our last time together, and we're too freaked out to be horny?"

I grab his arm. "What do you mean, our last time?"

"This is Reagan's bloodbath. They want to wipe us off the face of the earth." He pulls me back into his arms. "I know I screwed up at school, but this is the only place I ever felt I belonged. I want to be here with you when the shit comes down."

"I know exactly what you mean," I whisper. "It's like we have our own secret world, you and me. When I came here, it was the first time I ever felt like I was home, where I could be me without getting stomped on. Isla Vista is a special place, like Lothlorien, or Pepperland. That must be why they've come to destroy it."

Another big truck rumbles by outside, and a single nearby shot shatters the quiet.

"Oh, fuck—what was that?" Joel lunges off the bed, kneels down and feels around on the floor.

I sit up, pull my hair away from my face and let it hang down my back. I peer down at Joel on the floor. "What are you doing?"

"That shot was really close. Somebody might be hurt—" He grabs his pants and yanks them on. "Got to take a look." He runs out of the room.

It takes me a little longer to slip into my own jeans and T-shirt. I pad into the living room. Joel has pulled the couch aside and the door is wide open. He's out on the concrete porch that faces the driveway, looking out toward the street. I come up behind him and slip my arms around his waist. The cement is ice cold on my bare feet.

"Do you see anything?"

"No, nothing." He reaches back and pulls me closer. "I don't know what the hell that was."

We step back inside, close and lock the door. We make our way around the sofa and shove it against the door to block the way in. I go to the kitchen window that faces the street and part the curtains to look out. It's dark, but I think I could make out a body if one were lying in the street. I shiver as I let the curtains fall back.

In the living room, Joel turns on the radio. "...KCSB has been ordered, it has been dictated, whatever phrase you wish to use, KCSB has been told it must shut down immediately. We regret this deeply. We will not editorialize, although we feel very strongly about it. We will simply say that I consider it to be probably one of the most regrettable things I have ever heard to happen to this campus..."[3]

Joel and I stare at each other while the announcer closes down the station.

"Oh, shit!" he groans. "They shut down the radio station so nobody'll know what they're doing. This really has become a police state!"

I'm reeling at the news. My legs feel wobbly and I put my hand on the wall to steady myself. My whole insides feel like ice. "You... you know what this means." I can hardly get the words out. "It means they really have killed people."

"Yeah. But we already knew that." There's nothing but dead air on the radio and Joel switches it off.

"I knew it, but I didn't know it," I try to explain. "Some part of me hoped the guy they shot at the bank was just wounded."

He slips his arm around my shoulders. "Come on. Lets crawl into bed and get warm."

We hold each other under the covers. He's cold, and I pull him on top of me. I wrap my arms around his back and stretch out my legs against his to warm him up. He slides his arms under me and we roll over sideways. I bury my face in his neck and shoulder and breathe in his faint musky scent as we hold each other.

"Hmmm... I think there's only one way we're going to get warm," he growls. He rolls onto his back with me on top of him and his hands move down to squeeze my butt, press it down. I raise myself on my elbows, and work my way down until he's inside.

Our lovemaking is desperate and tender. Afterwards, Joel says, "We probably won't even be alive a month from now."

"I know," I whisper.

He kisses me and gives my right butt cheek a playful squeeze. "Want to know what I call this?"

I giggle. "Uh... Righteous balling?"

"Well, yeah—it was most definitely that, wasn't it? Oh darling..." He strokes my face and hair with the utmost tenderness. "What I call it is playing in the apocalypse."

10

A SHOW OF FORCE

The little black and white cocker spaniel lies on the front lawn, his head and neck strained upward and sideways. The long fur on his side is soggy with blood. I run across the lawn and kneel beside him. I stroke the soft white fur on his hind leg. He's cold and stiff, his open eyes cloudy and glazed. Blood leaks from his mouth onto the wet, dewy grass. He belongs to the people who live a couple of houses up the street. His name is Frodo, and he never made it home.

"Oh, shit—I'm going to throw up!" Joel runs back inside.

Tears blur my eyes and trickle down my cheeks. "Oh Frodo, I'm sorry. I'm so, so sorry." I gulp back my sobs and try to straighten his lifeless head, but he's too rigid. We never thought to look for a dog last night; could we have saved him?

Back inside, I take a faded gold-colored bedspread off the closet shelf. Joel and I use it for a beach blanket. I carry it across the living room. June comes out of her bedroom in a robe made from two emerald and olive green velour towels sewn together.

"What's going on?"

I sink down onto the couch, swipe my hand across my eyes. "Oh June—they shot that little dog, Frodo. He's lying out there on our lawn, all bloody—fucking PIGS!"

June recoils as if I'd slapped her, gray eyes wide, almost all pupil. "Nooo!" Her mouth goes all distorted like a tragedy mask. She runs outside and I follow her. Together, we cover Frodo with the bedspread. Tears stream down our faces.

Someone touches my shoulder; Joel is back. His skin is pale with a grayish tinge. He smells like throw up. "Sorry I bailed on you."

"S'okay. I'd be sick too if I hadn't grown up with a dad that hunted." It's a good thing his parents got him out of the army.

"We've got to tell Kendall and Merrily," June says.

"Yeah. I guess we do." I take Joel's hand. The three of us make our way up the street. Dread makes our steps slow like a funeral march. June is still in her robe. At the pink stucco house where Frodo lived, we stand on the porch for a long moment while I gather my strength. I make myself push the doorbell button.

Kendall opens the door. He looks like Donovan with his mop of curly black hair and purple paisley shirt. He's wearing white sailor pants and those water buffalo sandals from India that have a loop for the big toe. "What's happening?"

"Really, really bad shit," I tell him. "We found Frodo on our front lawn this morning. Somebody shot him during the night."

"Uhhh..." Kendall shakes his head. He hooks his thumbs in his belt loops. "You're putting me on, right?"

We don't say anything. I don't have any more words, and I don't think anybody else does, either. Kendall stares at June's blotchy, tear-streaked face, then at me. My eyes feel scratchy and swollen; I must look awful. Joel looks pale and angry.

"Oh..." Kendall's face crumples and he bites his lip. His thumbs jerk out of his belt loops—his fists clench and he jams the knuckles of one hand against his teeth. "Show me where he is," he says at last, and we take him back to our front yard. We leave him sobbing as he wraps Frodo in the bedspread and gathers him up.

"What kind of a monster," June says when we're inside, "would shoot an innocent little dog?"

Joel and I were on our way to get the Bug when we found Frodo. Kendall is gone when we head out again, and we walk fast down the driveway. We do not look at the front lawn.

There is glass on the asphalt from the shattered street lights. Some of the cars parked along the street are sitting on rims surrounded by torn rubber; their tires have been shot. Joel grips my hand, steeling himself for what we will find, but the Bug is parked next to a thick hedge, its tires still intact. Joel goes limp with relief. There's a shiny gouge on the back fender where the bullet scoured the paint off. He gives me a grim smile. "Battle scar," he says.

Joel forces his way sideways between the hedge and the driver's door and gets in. He pops the lock on the passenger door and I open it, dust some sand off the seat, and sit down. He turns the key in the ignition and the car hums into life.

Joel drives around the loop and parks just off Embarcadero on Seville, one of the side streets leading to the campus. We get out of the car and walk to the bank, which looks undamaged other than a couple of boarded-up windows. Tear gas canisters, rocks, and broken glass litter the street. Joel kicks one of the empty canisters and it clatters across the pavement like a tin can.

We stroll past the Unicorn Bookstore to the pool hall. Joel's old roommate Dan stands at a table shooting some balls.

"What the fuck happened last night?" Joel asks. "I drove in after work and it was like a war zone."

"Don't you know?" Dan sets his cue down on the green felt. "This guy Kevin Moran got shot. He was dead by the time the ambulance got him to the hospital. The crazy thing is, he and some other guys were actually *defending* the bank. Police totally deny that they shot him, but they came roaring in with their big dump trucks, surrounded the bank, and cops came pouring out with their rifles... and that's right when he got shot. I'd say it's pretty clear." He swipes a long, straw-colored lock out of his eyes. Joel stares at Dan's shoulder-length ringlets and his hand creeps up to touch his own shorn hair. His mouth flattens, and a bitter look crosses his face.

"KCSB had a reporter in Borsodi's," I say, "right across the street from the bank."

"After they shot this guy, Kevin something or other," Joel begins. He swipes his hand through his hair, pushes it back from his forehead.

"Kevin Moran," Dan breaks in. He picks up the cue and leans over the table.

"Yeah, Moran," Joel goes on, "then they shut KCSB down." He slams his hand down on the edge of the table. "Totally illegal."

"Yeah," Dan says. "That way, nobody outside could find out what they were doing. They took full advantage of that opportunity—" he points the cue at one of the balls and sights along its length, one eye closed. "Spent the rest of the night wreaking havoc—what they call a show of force." He taps the ball and it rolls into a corner pocket.

Joel and Dan talk about the shooting, and I wander over to the window. A student, a dog… who else died last night? Outside, a patrol car cruises by and I shove my hands in my pockets to keep from giving it the finger. Dan says the police claim Kevin was shot by snipers on rooftops with high-powered rifles—yeah, right!

I cross my arms over my chest and hug myself tight. Everything feels off kilter. My whole world has changed. It feels like only yesterday that my biggest worries were things like *What am I gonna wear? Do I look fat? Why didn't he call?* —and *I'll never get this paper done!* I still believed we all had guaranteed constitutional rights—freedom of speech, freedom of the press… The KCSB shutdown was a horrible awakening. When 91.5 FM died, I was stunned. I never knew that could happen here.

I sit in the pillow corner with my books. Joel and Dan went surfing, but I begged off; I have to memorize and recite the first part of the prologue to Chaucer's Canterbury Tales in Middle English next Wednesday morning in Professor Frost's office.

"Whan that Aprill with his shoures soote

The droghte of March hath perced to the roote,

And bathed every veyne in swich licour

Of which vertu engendred is the flour…"[1] is how it begins. The English language has changed a lot!

Written in the late 1300s, *Canterbury Tales* is a long poem about a group of folks on holy pilgrimage to the shrine of Saint Thomas a Becket, the martyred Archbishop of Canterbury. To pass the time, each of the pilgrims tells a story. The tales range from courtly love to rape, corrupt public officials, and a crude, hilarious yarn about adultery, farting, and a red hot poker. The kinds of stories people tell have *not* changed.

Will and June come out of her bedroom. "We're going out for a walk," June says. "Last chance before that hideous curfew starts—come with us!"

"No, I really have to get this done. Have fun," I say.

"Can we get you anything?" Will asks.

"No, but thanks."

June's blue paisley skirt swishes as they leave. I stare at the closing door. In just a little while we'll be on lockdown again. What a dodo bird not to get outside while I can! But I'm alone in the apartment now—I can practice out loud! I'm way too embarrassed to recite that poem in front of other people. I get to my feet.

"Whan that Aprill with his shoures soote…" I pace back and forth while I recite; let the rhythm take me over, swing my arms, do a couple of dance steps. "The hooly blisful martir for to seke that hem hath holpen whan that they were seeke…" [2]

Behind me, the door closes. "Far fucking out!"

I spin around. I feel my face flush hot. Oh no! It's Joel. He steps into the living room and leans his surfboard against the wall. The sandy wetsuit draped over his arm falls to the carpet. He's barefoot, in raggedy old jeans and a grubby white T-shirt.

"Oh, hi!" I say. I dig my big toe into the carpet.

"What was that? Sounds like some weird hobbit language." He steps into the kitchen, takes a glass from the cupboard, and fills it at the sink.

"It's Middle English," I say. "Can you believe I have to recite that out loud and get it right or I'll flunk the class?" I get the book from the pillow corner and show him.

"Wow—this is gnarly!" Joel gulps his water. "What does it mean?"

"Oh, something like 'When April's sweet showers end March's drought and bathe every vein with the sap that causes flowers to bloom,' and so on. It's a description of spring, and people coming from all over to visit a shrine in Canterbury. I feel like a total basket case trying to pronounce it."

"No way." He drains his glass and sets it on the counter. "Do it again—start over. It's so cool! I want to hear the whole thing."

"Well, okay. Whan that Aprill…" I don't dance around this time.

Joel follows along in the book while I recite. "Perfect!" he exclaims when I come to the end. As if he'd know.

It's evening and Joel is in the shower. June and I are at the kitchen window watching dump trucks full of police barrel down the street. "Will!" June calls. "Come look at this."

Will pads into the kitchen in sock feet. His white shirt has come untucked from his brown corduroy pants. He stands next to June, his arm around her waist. "Holy shit. Look at those guns!"

"I'm going to call my parents," I say. "Let them know what's going on, just in case."

"I already told mine," June says, "after they shot Frodo. I wish I hadn't—they want me to drop out of school and come home."

I sink down on the vinyl seat of one of the metal chairs, fingers pressed against my cheeks. "Oh, fuck! What did you say?"

"I said, 'No way am I leaving!'" She tugs Will's arm. "Come on, babe." They amble out of the kitchen.

I stare at the phone on the counter. Should I call? What if they show up and try to make me leave—start the semester over at some place like San Jose State? But I have to call; it's the right thing to do. It would be really cruel not to when the next news they have of me might be from the coroner. I get up and step over to the counter, pick up the receiver, and listen to the dial tone for a minute before I make the call... They shut down the radio station. What if they cut the phone lines next?

Mother answers. "Hello?" Her voice is sweet and girlish in case I'm one of her church friends. Their beige phone hangs on the varnished wood dining room wall.

"Hi, it's me." I tell her what the police are doing, how they shot a student. I describe the big dump trucks, how they're like tanks. "They gunned down our neighbor's dog—"

"No," she interrupts me. "You're mistaken. You're being taken in—it's all lies. It's just a Communist plot to make our Government look bad." Has she sat down in the chair they keep next to the phone? Or is she pacing back and forth in her terry cloth slippers?

"But I've *seen* it! It's happening outside right now!" I hold the phone up to the window. "Listen—that's one of their trucks going by." Gunfire rings out somewhere, maybe a block away.

"I don't hear anything," Mother says. "Besides, if anything like that was happening, it would be in the news."

She doesn't believe me! It's as if her fist has come out of that receiver and punched me, and I reel back from the counter. The cord pulls and the phone slides over the edge, but I lunge forward and grab it just in time. It's as if my own experience doesn't exist—as if *I* don't exist. An icy ball forms in my stomach where the punched feeling is and the chill spreads up into my arms and throat. This is the way I imagine it was in Nazi Germany. A lot of people who had Jewish friends still adored their Fuhrer; they couldn't bear to know the truth, so they just convinced themselves it wasn't really happening.

"You let your imagination run away with you," Mother goes on. "You always have. It's time to grow up and start living in the real world."

I lean over the counter. I want to slam that phone down so bad but I don't. "Okay," I say. "I just wanted to let you know what's going on. I've got to go now—bye."

The cold, punched feeling lingers, but now it feels bright and clean like a steel blade. I feel like I just woke up. The truth was always there, but I didn't let myself see it. My parents are not my friends. They're against everything that's important to me; everything I stand for. They will never be on my side. *Mother. She calls herself my mother...* How dare she talk to me like that?

I stride into the living room and slam my fist down on the brick-and-board bookshelf. June looks up from the pillow corner where she's reading. Inside her bedroom, Will sprawls on the bed with a magazine. In the bathroom, the shower stops and the shower curtain rings rattle as they slide along their metal rod.

"What?" June says. The only light in the room is a lamp perched on a cardboard box draped with a blue and green scarf so it looks like a table. It makes the tousled strands on top of her head glow like hot wires.

"I was just talking to my mom—this is insane! She and my dad won't believe what's happening. No news is getting out so they think I'm making it all up."

She sets her open book face down on a pillow. "Of course there's no news. Fascist pigs sealed us off and shut down the radio station."

"Yeah, but—" An idea bursts into my head like fireworks on the Fourth of July. "They haven't cut the phone lines yet. Let's call KRLA!"

"OUTTA SIGHT!" June jumps up and we bang shoulders together on the way to the kitchen. "We're the most far-out chicks in Isla Vista!" June dials the number of the Los Angeles rock 'n' roll station. She has it on a card next to the phone; she likes to call in dedications for Will when he's in LA. We hold the receiver between us so we can both talk.

"KRLA Radio."

"Are you the DJ doing the show tonight?" June's voice is excited and breathless, and we crowd together. Our sides touch. June feels warm. Real.

"That I am, sweetheart. Do you have a request for me?"

"No!" I blurt. "We're calling from Isla Vista. Terrible things are happening here, and nobody knows because the police shut down the radio station."

"Shut down the radio station? Is this for real? Wait a second—let me put you on the air," the DJ says... "Okay. Now start from the beginning."

We tell him about Kevin Moran's death, the rifles, the shotguns, the tear gas, the dump trucks, how they gunned down people's pets—everything. Joel comes in. "It's KRLA," I whisper to him.

He joins us at the phone. "The police themselves are doing all the rioting," he says. "Nobody's on the streets but the police—they called in the SWAT riot squad from Los Angeles. It is *so dark* here—they shot out all the street lights. They've sealed off the town, nobody can get in or out, and they shut down KCSB, the radio station."

"We need to get the word out," I say.

"You just did," says the DJ. "Thanks for calling, and best of luck!"

After June hangs up, I turn to Joel. "What's this about the LA riot squad? Where'd you find that out?"

"Surfers were talking about it at the beach." He stares at June and me. His face is dead serious as he switches off the kitchen light. "They may kill us for what we just did. We'd better lay low, stay away from the windows."

"The DJ never asked for our names," June argues. "They don't know who called."

He runs his fingers through his wet hair. "Makes no difference. They can seize the call records from KRLA and trace the number here."

June and I run through the apartment and close the curtains on all the windows—bedrooms, bathroom, kitchen, living room. In the bedroom doorway, Will leans against the doorjamb, one leg crossed over the other. "Did you guys have some kind of suicidal urge?" he drawls, stroking his pointed little Shakespeare goatee. Like a stage light, the lamp in the pillow corner throws his shadow against the wall.

Back in the kitchen, I rummage in the dark through the odds-and-ends drawer until I my fingers touch the package of white wax candles that came from the grocery store. I take them out and set them on the living room bookshelf next to the radio along with a book of matches. "Look what I found," I say. "Now we won't have to turn on any lights."

"Groovy." June lights a candle and turns off the lamp. She and I go back to the kitchen and fish beer bottles out of the trash to use as candle holders. We put candles in the bathroom and both bedrooms.

"I wonder how long it'll take for them to trace that call," I say.

"No idea." June shrugs. "I still think there's a pretty good chance they don't know—it's not like they're driving around in their trucks listening to KRLA."

Joel brings a blanket out of my room, climbs on the sofa, and drapes the heavy fabric over the curtain rod to black out any light that might escape. He gets down, looks up at his handiwork, and starts to laugh. "Jesus—I'm being a little paranoid, don't you think?"

"Yeah," Will says, "the 'noids, man. That's why I left my stash at home this weekend." We all burst out laughing.

I go back to the kitchen, take four beers from the fridge, and bring them to the living room. "I think we could use some refreshment."

We all sit on the floor, our backs against the sofa, out of the line of fire. The cold beer tastes wonderful.

Joel and I huddle together in bed, fully dressed in case the police break in during the night and drag us off to jail. Trucks and gunshots keep jarring us awake. I hear someone outside the bedroom window on the narrow strip of grass between the house and the row of arbor vitae. The curtain is closed tight—he can't see in. I lie still and don't make a sound. Joel is sleeping; he never knows.

When morning comes, I feel like I haven't slept at all. With all the drapes closed, the whole apartment is still dark. I look at the clock on my nightstand. In the gloom, I can barely make out the numbers but it's 7:30 already! I slip out of bed, tiptoe into the kitchen, and get the coffee started. While it's percolating, I open the curtains. Fog has rolled in during the night. I go outside and pad barefoot across the wet lawn and around the corner of the building. In the side yard, the grass is trampled, big soggy footprints under the bedroom windows. I wrap my arms around my chest and shiver.

Back in the kitchen, I sit at the table with a mug of coffee. My eyes feel gritty from lack of sleep, and I screw my fists into them. Joel comes in, tucking his rumpled blue workshirt into his jeans, and pours himself some coffee. He sits down across from me and spoons sugar into his cup.

"Surprise—we're still alive!" He grins and nudges my leg with his bare foot.

I crawl around on my hands and knees, gathering little round oak balls out of the grass underneath the scrubby live oak. The balls lie in my palm like dried peas; they're brownish gray and hard like wood, about half an inch wide. I don't know what they are. They can't be seeds; those are the acorns. I do know that we had them under the oak trees at home, too. I used to draw faces on them when I was little. Next to me, Joel looks up from the red paperback of Yeats's poems that I loaned him. I brought *The Dharma Bums* by Jack Kerouac but I haven't opened it yet. The sun has burned off the fog, and it's a warm afternoon. I roll off my knees and sit cross-legged next to Joel.

"Let me borrow your pen," I say.

Joel pulls a ball-point from his left shirt pocket and hands it to me.

"Thanks!" The pen makes a satisfying *snick* when I push the button to make the point come down. On one of the oak balls, I draw eyes, a nose, and what started out to be kissy lips but ends up being a blob.

Joel is absorbed in his book. "God—this guy's stuff is fucking incredible!"

"I knew you'd like him." I make a cat face on the next oak ball; then I get lazy. I draw simple smiling faces on the rest. I open my hand and let them fall to the ground. Ballpoint pen ink is permanent. Maybe someone will sit here, months or a year from now, and pick up an oak ball. What a surprise to see a face smiling up at you! What if the person is falling apart, even suicidal, and that little smiling face is the thing that turns his whole life around? That's something Ray in *The Dharma Bums* would think… I pick up the book and open it. I'm at the part where Ray rides freight trains and camps out on the beach. He calls himself a bhikku, a wandering Buddhist monk. His friend

Japhy Ryder lives in a cabin on a hill with grass mats, a Chinese inscription on the door, and papers with Chinese calligraphy and his own poems tacked all over the burlap wallpaper. Japhy makes people take their shoes off when they come inside. He sits on a mat with his pot of Chinese tea and sips the brew while he writes poems. The book sucks me in all the way. I yearn for that cabin—Kerouac makes it sound like bliss.

I long to be a dharma bum. I want to stand on the road with my thumb out and go all over the place, make long treks into the wilderness, and write everything down while I sip tea from a handleless cup like a little bowl... But how can I leave Joel? I walk around like an empty shell all week when he's working in LA. The guys in Kerouac's books keep their girlfriends on the edges of their lives; they don't get attached. They go off whenever they feel like it and leave their lovers behind. It would be a huge wrench for me to go on the road without Joel, but I'll graduate in June, and then it will be time to leave. Where can I go? What if I apply for a fire lookout job and spend the summer on an isolated mountain peak just like Jack Kerouac? Do they even hire women for those jobs? Surf spots are the only places Joel wants to go. He'd go nuts in the mountains.

I look up from the page. On the other side of the park, a police car drives by. Yeats' poetry has captured Joel; his finger traces the lines and his lips move as he savors every word... I need to savor every single moment we have together, not agonize over the future. We may not even be alive tomorrow.

The last time I got groceries, I saw Japanese tea sets with a bamboo-handled teapot and four little cups for sale at the Isla Vista Market.

"Joel," I say, and hold out the pen.

He looks up. Our fingers touch as he takes it from me. He puts it back in his shirt pocket. "Done making notes in your book?"

"Nah." I close the book and straighten my crossed legs. "I was just dinking around making faces on oak balls. I need to go over to IV Market and get a Japanese teapot."

"Yeah?" He closes his book too.

"The guys in this book were sitting on straw mats sipping their tea and writing poems," I explain. "I want to do that too."

"I'll go with you." He gets to his feet, dusts bits of grass off his pant legs. He reaches down to me. "Come on."

I take his hand and he pulls me up. "Oh Joel, I wish you didn't have to leave."

"Yeah. Me, too!"

We hold hands as we stroll across the grassy open space and pass other people enjoying these last hours outdoors before curfew. Some sit on the grass with their books spread out around them; others just chat. Patrol cars cruise around the loop at the edge of the park. Joel and I amble up Embarcadero del Mar to the market. It looks like a country store with clapboard siding and lots of signs: Arden Milk, Pepsi Cola, and Bubble-Up. We go inside. The screen door bangs shut behind us.

The dark wood floorboards squeak as we walk past Campbell's soup cans, Rice-a-Roni, Duncan Hines muffin mixes, and corn flakes to the kitchen section over by the window. There are dishes, pans, silverware—and Japanese tea sets that come packed in a cardboard box with Japanese characters.

We buy the tea set and a package of jasmine tea. I stuff them into my turquoise blue and white Greek cotton shoulder bag along with our books. "Let's walk over to Taco Bell," I say. "I'm dying for a green burrito."

The bank parking lot is full of sheriff's and Highway Patrol vehicles. The officers have lined up in front of the bank to protect it from a crowd that has gathered.

"You dudes keep talking about snipers," somebody yells. "Well, I sure don't see any picking *you* off—where are they?"

"Only fuckin' gunmen in this town are the po-leese!" another voice bellows.

"I changed my mind," Joel says. "No way am I leaving you alone here. I'll drive back home in the morning—I'll still have plenty of time to get to work."

I slip my arm around his waist. "I'm so glad!" I lean against him. "Can you guess what I'm thinking?"

"I can't imagine." A laugh bubbles up and he grins. "But *I'm* thinking we never got a chance to ball last night."

I punch his arm. "That's exactly what I was thinking!"

We walk past the bank to Perfect Park. A few people stand on the grass, their eyes on the crowd, waiting. We wait too. We all stand together in a shimmering bubble where time is suspended in an eternal moment. The sun is low in the sky and casts a golden glow over each person. There's a blonde girl in a white Mexican peasant blouse, hair pulled back in a loose ponytail next to a guy in jeans and black T-shirt; a couple of straight-looking, short-haired frat guys in khaki pants and Ban-Lon knit shirts; a girl in pants with green, white and brown stripes; a rugged-looking mountain man with long, honey-colored hair and a full beard—they waver in the orange light like a reflection in water. They shimmer. Just for an instant they are almost transparent, frozen in a moment that will never come again. A beam of sunlight hits the oak tree, turning the leaves a bright, iridescent green and bathing a spider web suspended between two branches in a metallic glow, gone when the sun sinks a bit lower. I get a lump in my throat. We are all so precious and so fragile.

The whap-whap-whap of helicopter blades in the distance chops the air into tiny pieces. It gets louder and builds to a deafening roar. The bubble winks out and time rushes back in. Up the street, the dump trucks are coming fast from all directions. The engines rev and shift gears, faster and faster. Joel grabs my hand and we head across the park toward home. Behind us, the trucks careen down the street and fire tear gas at the crowd around the bank. The helicopter roars overhead and drops tear gas into the park. We all break into a run. We cross the far end of the park and dash down Trigo, past Sun and Earth, into clean air. We slow down to a fast walk. Joel's hands are over his mouth. He coughs, over and over. "Wow!" he gasps. "So that was tear gas—man, is it fucked!"

I cough and wheeze. I wipe my eyes. "Yeah. I can't believe they dropped it out of the helicopter."

We come to the end of the block and jag down Pescadero to Sabado Tarde. The streets away from the loop are quiet, and we make it home before the dump trucks start patrolling the residential area.

We burst into the apartment and rush to the kitchen sink where we splash our faces with cold water from the faucet. June watches from the kitchen doorway.

"Oh God—did you guys get gassed?"

"Yep. They're dropping it from a helicopter!" I grab the teakettle off the stove and fill it. I switch on the burner and get the water started for tea. "Looks like Will made it out okay?"

"He took off a couple of hours ago," she says. "Well, Joel, looks like you're stuck here for the night."

"Yeah, I'll split in the morning," he says. He dries his face with a dishtowel, crumples it up, and leaves it on the counter. "I'd better call my parents, let them know I won't be there tonight."

I take my new tea set out of its box and give the pot and cups a good washing. They are mottled brown stoneware with abstract, dark blue brushwork on the sides that might be a Japanese character, but I can't tell. June watches, slouched against the counter, her weight all on one leg, the other crossed over with just her toes touching the floor. I get a clean towel out of the drawer and dry the teapot. June touches the bamboo handle. "This is so pretty! Where did you find it?"

"Would you believe, the IV Market?" I pick up a cup and wipe it dry. "I wonder if this design means anything."

"Maybe it's the character for tea?" she guesses. I put some jasmine tea leaves in the pot and set it on the stove to wait until the water is almost boiling. I gather up Joel's and my towels and take them to the clothes hamper in the bathroom. I put fresh candles in the beer bottles we used last night and light them. I flip through the stack of records that lean against the living room wall until I find Ravi Shankar. I start the record and the sitar and tabla fill the room with music that is as far away from guns and dump trucks as I can imagine.

In the kitchen, Joel is on the phone. June puts chocolate chip cookies on a plate. I pour boiling water into the teapot. I carry the pot and three cups into the living room and set them on the coffee table. June brings the cookies and we sit on the couch. She kicks off her Birkenstocks and I wiggle my feet out of their Capezios.

In a few minutes, Joel joins us. He squeezes in between us and I pour him a cup of tea. He leans back, takes a sip and looks around. "Thanks," he says. "God, this is nice. I'm so glad I'm here and not driving to LA tonight."

"We are totally into your being here," June says. "Great music, Kate—I wouldn't have thought to pick it but it really changes the whole vibe."

I hadn't thought about how scared June might be with Will gone. "Thanks," I say. "I hope it masks the noise outside."

June pushes herself up from the sofa and crosses the carpet to her room. She comes back with a stick of incense and lights it with the candle on the bookcase. Queen of the Night drifts through the air as she sits back down.

Joel bites into a cookie, chews, and swallows. "I talked to my dad," he says. "Told him what's happening." He gulps more tea. "Dad thinks your phone is tapped, so be careful what you say."

June and I both turn and stare at him. "What?" I say. "How would he know?"

"That was his job in the war—he specialized in communications. He says there are strange clicks on your line, like it's connecting to more than one place."

"Oooohhh," June says. "They want to make sure we don't call any more radio stations."

"So KRLA ratted us out," I say. "Figures."

"Probably didn't have any choice," Joel says.

June has a grim smile on her face. "Huh. Are we fuckin' heroes, or what?"

We three sit together on the couch and keep each other company all evening. Candlelight makes the room cozy. We do our best not to pay attention when the dump trucks go by; we try not to listen when the shots ring out. Incense and Ravi Shankar take us far away. We take turns reading Shakespeare sonnets, Byron, and Shelley.

All through the dark night, Joel and I hold each other. This could be our last time together. I know every time could be our last, but tonight it feels so real. The Doors' song, "The End,"[3] plays over and over again in my head. We make love as if the world is ending, as if it's our last chance.

11

THE ISLA VISTA COMMUNITY GARDEN

They're lined up along the edge of the park in their red burlap robes, heavy ox yokes around their necks, black ash like charcoal smeared across their foreheads. Their eyes are fixed on some faraway point, perhaps a distant cloud, and do not waver. Their faces are stern. The afternoon sun streams down and sweat beads their flushed faces, especially the women in their biblical head coverings. The men are bareheaded. They carry heavy wooden staves in one hand; with the other they hold up hand-lettered cloth signs like scrolls.

"Warning!!! Turn your eyes toward Memphis (Egypt), for out of it shall come the great confusion."[1]

"Oh daughter of my people, gird thee with sackcloth and wallow thyself in ashes. Make thee mourning as for an only son, most bitter lamentation, for the spoiler shall suddenly come upon us."[2]

I nod when I read that sign. For sure, the "spoiler" has already come to this community.

A gust of wind makes the signs flutter like pillowcases on a clothesline. That old saying, "It's an ill wind that blows no good," whips through my brain. I stop and wipe my sweaty hands on my pant legs. My feet swelter in their stiff new leather Redwing boots. I look up at the line of people in their itchy-looking, scratchy robes. Can these apocalyptic figures be real? Or are they personifications of all our thoughts, the rage that percolates and simmers underneath everything we do, when we go to the market, ride our bicycles, sit in our classes, prepare our meals, and try to study? The cops haven't arrested them—how can they be real? Police are a constant presence—they have seized our town and inhabit it like occupying forces. They sneer at us through the windows of their patrol cars while the war goes on and on.

Nixon bypassed all the checks and balances and unilaterally invaded Cambodia. Protests have erupted all over the nation, and in the crackdown, four students were shot dead at Kent State, two at Jackson State. Countless others were injured. The country is in the hands of a renegade government.

I hardly know this place anymore, it has changed so much. No more carefree dancing in the street—everything feels heavy now. Weighted down. Sad.

I go up to the man on one end of the line. His robe is wrinkled, as though it had been wadded up and stuffed into a bag before he put it on. There's a scratch on the back of his hand gripping the stave. "Who are you guys?" I ask. "Where did you come from?"

He doesn't look at me. None of them do. They don't move. They don't say a word.

My boot soles scuff the pavement and I lift my feet higher as I walk past them. Their signs all scream dire warnings about the end of a corrupt, greedy nation, full of abominations. Maybe they're trying to scare everyone so we'll join their Jesus freak cult, but for me, their robes, their signs, and their grim faces all mirror the outrage we feel being under the giant fist of Reagan's "spoiler" police. At the other end of the row is a folding chair with a shoebox full of leaflets and a sign: "Free! Take one!" I pick up one of the pamphlets and open it.

"The Prophets of Doom of 'The Children of God' in dramatic demonstrations across the nation are warning of the death of the nation in the red sackcloth of mourning, the yoke of bondage and the rod of judgment and bearing the scrolls of prophesy. In thundering silence they have stood in vigil between the violence of revolution and the sins of the system from White House to capital, UN to cathedral, and from coast to coast!"[3]

I turn and stare at them. They're real, all right. Now that I think about it, my own mind would never have created those sackcloth robes and yokes. I would've come up with something more like the grim reaper or a medieval executioner. I picture them gripping axes instead of wooden staves; the curved blades gleam like the ones in my worst nightmares, and I grow cold inside. I quicken my steps.

Farther down the loop is a bus. Affixed to its side is a big sign: "The Prophet Bus. Get on for free food, music, love."

I walk right past.

These boots are so heavy. My legs ache; every step is an effort. My flimsy kid leather Capezios and light sandals have in no way prepared me for these tough Redwing boots. They have thick rubber soles with deep grooves for traction. I bought them in Santa Barbara last week. I want to go on mountain treks and leap from boulder to boulder without slipping just like Japhy and Ray in *The Dharma Bums*. I had no idea that even walking to my classes would feel like my feet were encased in cement blocks! It'll be a long time before I'm leaping.

It's a sunny Saturday morning in the community garden. The earth is damp and soft from the spring rains. About twenty people have come to loosen the soil and plant seeds. I spot some tools lying on the ground: a pick and a couple of rakes and hoes. All the shovels are already taken, and I choose the pick. It feels so good to swing it! I thonk it down and make big gouges in the earth—this is real, not some head trip the way discussing literature is. The end of the pick sinks deep into the soil and a surge of satisfaction wells up in my chest. I can't stop grinning.

I spot Velvet and Cyril in another part of the garden where the soil is already dug up. They're planting corn and cucumbers. I work on getting more ground ready, using the pick to yank up big chunks of grass and weeds and soften up the ground.

There's a little park across the street, and a rock band, The Travel Agency, is setting up its equipment. People come and sit on the grass, waiting. My pick is getting heavy. Guitars get tested, there are a few muffled drumbeats and at last, the fast opening riff of "Sorry You Were Born" rings out. I feel a burst of new energy and swing my pick in time to the music.

Velvet finishes planting her packet of seeds and picks up a shovel that another worker has abandoned. She stomps it down into the ground and lifts out a great clod of dirt. She got a brand-new pair of hiking boots the day after I got mine.

By midday, the sun beats down on us. A truck drives up and two older guys get out and lug several jugs of apple juice and a box of chocolate chip cookies across the dirt and set them down next to the tools. Everyone stops working. I open a jug of apple juice. It slides down my throat like ambrosia, and I grin at our benefactors in T-shirts and cutoff jeans. They're English Department professors, Dr. Wallach and Dr. Cousins. Who would have thought?

I think I'm the only person who came alone. Joel is not here. He said he could think of nothing worse than gardening and went surfing instead. All the other people working in the garden are couples, and there's a wistful ache in my chest. Wouldn't it be fine to have an old man who'd work with me in the garden? What we're doing feels so important. It's hard work and my arm and back muscles ache but it feels good to be using my body for something worthwhile. I shrug the kinks out of my shoulders and take my juice over to Velvet. I pass her the jug.

"This is beautiful," I say. "Wouldn't you love to have a garden out in the country and live from it entirely?"

She lifts the jug and takes a long swig. "I wouldn't want to depend on it entirely." As usual, Velvet is practical. Her brown eyes have a worried look as they meet mine. "What if the crop failed? They sometimes do, you know."

I take a big bite of cookie and stomp the dirt from my boot soles. "I don't think it would fail," I say. "But in the evenings by the fire, I'd be doing some kind of crafts to sell—leather work, embroidery... I could depend on that if I had to."

Velvet grins. "What about Joel? What'll he be doing?" She hands the jug back to me.

I take a big swig and wipe my mouth with the back of my hand. "I don't know," My voice comes out small and uncertain. I stare at her. She's got a dark purple bandanna tied around her head and her cheeks are flushed. She's getting sunburned. "It's so weird. We have the *best* conversations—it's like we take the words out of each other's mouths. It's as if we're linked. We've made our own private world. But we don't want the same kind of life. I'm digging the shit out of what we're doing today, and he said he couldn't think of anything worse."

"Wow!" Velvet frowns. "But if you never dig in the soil and plant stuff, you'll always be one step removed from what you eat." She flings her hands out sideways. "You won't even experience it fully."

"Exactly... only, it's not that simple." I hug the bottle against my chest. "Everything I'm getting out of this, he gets when he goes surfing. The ocean is what connects him."

"Oh dear." Velvet frowns. "Somehow I don't see you as a surfer."

"No shit. I'm not even a good swimmer." I stare at the ground and drag my boot toe through the dirt. "I don't know what's going to happen with us. He doesn't want the same things I do, but I can't imagine being without him."

"Then I think you're going to have to decide what's most important to you. Is it love? I mean the love you and Joel have now." She bends over and picks up her shovel. "Or is it having adventures on the road and living off the land?"

I don't want to think about such a huge dilemma right now. "They're all really important," I say. "I don't know which is most crucial." But I'm lying. Hands down, love is the most important, and who will ever love me the way Joel does? Women give up their dreams and live shadow lives for the sake of love.

I go back to swinging my pick harder than ever. A strong, brown hand at the end of a sinewy, hairy forearm snakes across from behind me and grips the wooden handle. I spin around—it's Dr. Wallach. He grins at me.

"Ah," he says. "The girl from my Lawrence seminar." His balding dark hair is cut so short that his scalp shows through. Intense dark eyes look out from under heavy black eyebrows. He has a big hooked nose, a wide mouth, and a strong square chin. Last year, I spent the whole D.H. Lawrence class wondering what it would be like to go to bed with him. He tugs the pick away from me. "Let me have that." He hands me a rake instead.

I rake out clumps of grass and put them in a big pile for compost. While I work, I watch Wallach out of the corner of my eye. He turns over more earth with that pick in half an hour than I did in a whole morning. Raw male energy radiates out of him, just as it did in his class, even though some of the asshole things he said freaked me out...

In *The Rainbow*, Ursula, a schoolteacher, beat a boy who had given her a lot of trouble. She felt degraded afterwards—because she had resorted to violence, I thought. That made it an empty victory. But Wallach had a different take on the scene.

"Ursula," he said, "has lost her womanhood by taking on a masculine role." He paced back and forth in front of the chalkboard, open book in one hand, making sweeping gestures with the other. "The boy here represents the masculine principle and she has beaten him down—a masculine action. This is why she feels degraded. Her being a schoolteacher is in itself unnatural—it is a masculine role."

Wallach found a woman like this in almost every book. Another favorite theme of his was childbirth.

"A woman's sex drive is different from a man's," he told the class. "A man finds fulfillment in the act of intercourse, but a woman cannot. Sexual fulfillment for a woman comes only in the act of childbirth."

The other women in the class confirmed this with solemn nods. What in the world? Were they all frigid or something? How dare this guy tell me what I felt or didn't feel? I got plenty of enjoyment out of sex… and even while I resented the piss out of him for his smug chauvinistic pronouncements, I couldn't stop imagining sex with him. My mind wandered away from the discussion about D. H. Lawrence, and I pictured us in a bedroom in a Santa Barbara tract house, sipping peach brandy.

This was how it would be. I'd stare into his deep-set eyes and he would reach for my blouse and rip it off with one powerful motion. We'd tear each other's clothes off, fabric ripping, buttons popping. It would be like tearing the wrapping off a Christmas present. He would have black hair all over his chest and belly… I squirmed in my seat. I nearly moaned aloud in class as I pictured the whole thing. I got so lost in my fantasy that I didn't realize the class was over and everybody had left except Wallach, who was putting his books in his briefcase. He always brought at least a dozen books to class.

"Time to wake up," he said. "Whatever was on your mind must have been pretty interesting."

I gave him what I hoped was a wistful, womanly smile. "I was thinking about how it would be to give birth to a child," I said.

He looked pleased. "I'm sure you'll have one some day." His voice was warm, kind. "D.H. Lawrence affects a lot of women that way."

I rake out one last clump of grass and drop it in the pile. I put the rake down. I have blisters on my palms and I gaze at my hands with pride. Some day they will be strong and calloused.

Wallach is smoothing the soil with a shovel and making depressed rows for seeds. He moves with casual ease; he's done this before. If he and I lived on a farm together, he'd be a real partner, except he'd probably expect me to stick to cooking and canning and washing his clothes—all the indoor stuff. I tear my eyes away—what makes him so sexy? There's his energy, his earthy magnetism; but it's more than that. He's a grown man, an adult male.

It's late afternoon. Velvet, Cyril, and I go across the street to join the gathering in the park. About 200 people sit and sprawl on the grass. The three of us sit down as the pure notes of a long guitar solo wash over us. Bottles of Gallo and Red Mountain are everywhere. A jug of vin rose is making the rounds. When it comes to me, I take a long swig, then another before I pass it on. It takes the ache out of my body and my stiff muscles unclench. I unlace my boots and tug them off. I peel off my sweaty socks and wiggle my toes. These park gatherings are one of the things I'll miss the most when it's time to leave IV. It's amazing that the police haven't come with their tear gas, but in the daytime, they concentrate their heavy patrols on the loop area near the bank and other businesses. We're blocks away— I'll bet they don't know we're here. For these few hours, we've had our community back. It's been like the old days and my throat swells. My eyes get misty—I'm so homesick for the way it was.

I stretch out my legs, lean back on my hands. The band plays through their repertoire of songs for the third time. Cyril gets up and pulls Velvet to her feet. "We're going to split now," he says.

I just nod and smile. "Take care."

I stay, lost in the music until Joel comes to find me.

12

PLEASURE FAIRE

Sometime during the night, someone pitched a gorgeous tent like a sheik's portable desert palace in the field across El Colegio road. It's made of purple velvet and red and gold brocade with three peaks on its roof that stretch toward heaven. In the morning sun, the fabric shimmers. I think of Aladdin and his lamp, Ali Baba and the forty thieves, and Ozma of Oz. The tent stands in a place of its own apart from the rows of awnings and vendor's booths that fill most of the field. It's the annual Isla Vista Pleasure Faire. On a wooden platform under a tree, the raspy-voiced lead singer of Alexander's Timeless Bloozband belts out "Love So Strong" while a harmonica wails.

Joel points to the red, purple, and gold tent. "I wonder what *that* is."

I lean against him and he slips his hand into my back pocket.

"It's like something in a fairy tale," he says.

"It's magical," I agree. "I think it just winked into existence. It looks holy. Let's go check it out."

Holding hands, we approach the tent. The heavy fabric door flap opens and a man who could be the biblical King David steps out. A circlet of braided leather like an everyday crown holds his reddish gold hair in place. His red beard is trimmed to about an inch. He has a big nose with flaring nostrils and piercing blue eyes that take in everything about us as we walk across the field. He wears a green robe belted at the waist and hand-made leather sandals on his feet.

King David all the way—I wonder if the Ark of the Covenant is in that tent.

"Greetings and welcome!" the man exclaims.

Joel bows. I do a clumsy curtsey with his hand still in my pocket.

The kingly man spreads his arms in a sweeping gesture. "And what, fair lady, does my tent look like to you?"

"A religious monument," I whisper. "A temple."

"Come in and see." The man holds the door flap open for us and we step inside. Medieval-looking leather goods of all kinds are spread out on wooden tables—belts, purses, sandals, hair ornaments, knife sheaths, and sword scabbards. "This is my shop," the man says. "I make things here, so it is indeed a religious monument because making things is sacred."

A petite woman in a red brocade dress steps out from behind a fabric curtain between this room and the back of the tent. An impossible mop of brown curls frames her face and cascades down her shoulders. Stepping into this tent is like going back in time, stepping back into the old stories. Joel and I in our jeans and T-shirts are centuries out of time.

"We have visitors, Esther," the man says.

She grins at him and at us. "Welcome," she says. "My husband Solomon made all these things." She sweeps her arms out wide. "Aren't they great?"

Joel and I go from table to table. "This stuff is really beautiful," I say. How can we not buy something? I just hope we can afford it; with all the hand tooling, it's going to be really expensive.

Esther holds out a leather barrette. "This would look beautiful in your hair. I really envy you your hair, so silky and straight."

What a blowmind. To me, my hair is boring. It just hangs there. "I've always wished I had curly hair like yours!" I take the barrette; it's hand tooled with a floral pattern. "I love this. How much is it?"

Esther and Solomon laugh. "Take it! It is absolutely free!" Solomon booms.

"We have a tradition," Esther explains. "Wherever we go, we gift something to our first visitors. It brings us luck." She hands Joel a belt with a brass buckle in the shape of a lion's head. How did she know he's a Leo?

"Wow! Are you sure?" Joel stares at them, then the belt, lips parted, eyes wide. I know he would have bought that belt anyway, he's so into being a Leo.

"Yes! Take them," Solomon grins at us. "Our first visitors are sent to us by God. What we give you is our gift to Him."

I put the barrette in my hair while Joel tucks in his shirt and threads the belt through the loops on his Levi's. "Thank you," he says. "We will never forget this."

"We'll tell everybody about what far out stuff you have," I add.

Solomon opens a couple of panels in the tent and makes a big door... The store is open. People are already coming toward us across the field.

Joel and I munch hot dogs loaded with sauerkraut and mustard as we wander among the booths selling India print skirts and dresses and plain shirts with embroidery.

"What am I doing in school?" I mutter to Joel. "I could make stuff like this."

We pass a booth with colorful bead necklaces.

"You could make these, too!" Joel grins and fingers the beads I made him, all in sea blues and greens with a tiki that looks like it came from Easter Island.

We pass a booth with wooden flutes at the end of the row and step out into the open. Our hot dogs are getting soggy from the sauerkraut and Joel throws the rest of his on the ground. Crows approach and squawk at each other. One grabs the end of the wiener. Another one flies away with the bun. I feel sorry for the ones who didn't get any and tear the rest of my hot dog into little pieces and toss them on the grass so they'll at least get something. I hate for anyone to be left out.

A warm wind gusts through the eucalyptus trees and the canvas awnings flap and tug at their skinny metal poles. On stage, congas and bass guitar make the air pulsate, like a heartbeat. The aroma of frying donuts mixed with the pungent, oily smell of eucalyptus trees fills the air.

Leather goods are for sale everywhere, but not the medieval-looking stuff Solomon and Esther had in their tent. I touch the new barrette in my hair. The texture of the design feels good on my fingertips.

"We really lucked out today," I say. "I can't believe those people actually *gave* us this stuff. Look at that belt you're wearing—you'll never find another one like it anywhere!"

"I know." Joel bends his head down to look at the buckle. "It's like he had me in mind the whole time he was making it. I'll bet he's some kind of wizard."

"I thought he was King David out of the Bible. But it's really the same thing. I expected there would be winged seraphim or gryphons or something in that tent."

"Yeah. Look around. This whole scene is totally medieval. I think we're traveling again."

All our imaginary journeys flood my mind... the day we first met when San Francisco turned into Italy, the time we found ourselves in the Australian outback... I'll never have this with anyone else. I grab his hand and squeeze it. How can I ever leave him?

We file past more booths: hats, ceramic bowls and cups, jewelry. We come to an Egyptian booth. I freeze, riveted. There are statues of Egyptian gods and goddesses, necklaces and bracelets like the pharaohs and their queens wore...

Joel picks up a little statue of a woman with the head of a cat. "This is totally you," he says. His wallet is in his hand. "We'll get this," he says.

The man starts to wrap it but I say, "Don't bother; I'll just hold it." The cat goddess *is* me. The tag says her name is Bast. Joel says I remind him of a Siamese cat, and Bast is the culmination of that.

With the statue in my hand, I hug Joel right there in front of the booth. "Thank you," I whisper. My cat tongue touches his earlobe.

Taj Mahal will be here tonight. I can't wait. I have two of his records, scratchy and worn out now because I've played them so much. I try not to think about the curfew that says we all have to be in our apartments before Taj even gets here. But we're on the other side of the street from Isla Vista proper so maybe they can't do anything as long as everyone stays here.

"We should get a bottle of wine before the concert," I tell Joel.

"Excellent idea." Holding hands, fingers laced together, we walk back to the duplex on Sabado Tarde. We're thirsty from the salty hot dogs we ate, and we get a bottle of apple juice from the fridge, grab muffins left over from breakfast, and take them out to the Bug.

Joel drives to the liquor store in Goleta. We buy our favorite, Japanese plum wine. With the wine in a paper bag, we head back on Hollister toward Isla Vista and turn on Los Carneros, where someone has taken the "Isla Vista" sign down and replaced it with "PRAGUE" in stark black letters.

Prague was overrun by Hitler's army. The General of Police, Karl Hermann Frank, announced over the radio that he would drown any uprising in a "sea of blood." There was an uprising. People built barricades but the German occupation forces retaliated with tanks and bombs and mowed down everyone who resisted.

Then in 1968, Czechoslovakia was attacked by the Soviet Union and other Warsaw Pact members. The Czechs had gotten too liberal, alarming the Soviets. Freedom of the press, open discussion, and freedom of speech prompted a brutal crackdown. Columns of tanks invaded Prague, and the whole country is still under occupation.

The faire is in the fields between Los Carneros and El Colegio Road. Parked cars line the streets, so Joel turns off on Camino del Sur and parks a couple of blocks away. He pulls his old beach blanket out of the back seat, folds it up, and puts it under his arm. I carry the muffins in a paper sack and stash the bottle of plum wine in my Greek shoulder bag.

We find an open spot in the grassy area in front of the stage. Joel spreads out the blanket and we sit down. I slip off my sandals and he takes off his tennis shoes. We dig our toes into the nubby surface of the blanket. The Travel Agency is on the stage playing one of their long instrumental numbers. The notes work their way into my muscles and bones and follow the nerve pathways until they fill my whole body with light. Is this what nirvana is like? I close my eyes and remember every light show from all the concerts I've been to, especially "Dry Paint" with its giant projections of Botticelli paintings in the midst of the flowing colors. Funny because I've only ever seen The Travel Agency outdoors, playing for free in the parks. But they're so good they make light shows in my mind. I open the bag of muffins and put it between us. Joel reaches in, takes one out, and tears off a big mouthful. He passes it to me; I take a bite and hand it back. I don't say anything, but what I'm dying for is a big plate of cheese enchiladas. I look back over my shoulder, crane my neck and check out the booths. No Mexican food. Oh well. It's getting dark when the music builds to a crescendo and the set is over. Thundering applause, loud whistles, people wanting more, but the band is unplugging their guitars and taking their instruments off the stage. Who is going to play next?

"I love that band," I say to Joel. "They've been giving free concerts ever since I came to IV."

"Yeah, they're really good," he says. "I'd like to get their record. Do they have one?"

"No. I can't imagine why."

Joel squooges around sideways and lies down with his head in my lap. My fingers play with his hair. I nibble on another muffin while we wait for the next band to get set up. It's peaceful but there's a tense feeling in the air; everyone keeps looking around, on the alert for police. I hope they don't come barreling into the field with flame throwers.

A short-haired guy in white pants and a Hawaiian shirt climbs onto the stage and steps over to the microphone. "Testing, testing... sorry, sorry. We've just gotten the news that Taj has canceled. We know this is a huge disappointment, really a bummer... we'll see who we can find at short notice for tonight's concert."

"Oh, fuck!" Joel sits up. "And you *know* why the son of a bitch cancelled. Doesn't want to be *involved!*"

"I don't blame him," I say. "Can't you just see those pigs hauling off Taj Majal? Huge black man, way over six feet tall? He would be a big trophy for them—shit, black people know all about police brutality."

Joel stares at me. "God, you're right."

"Whatever cop arrested him would probably get promoted," I say. "We could go home, play his records, have our own little Taj Mahal concert."

He shakes his head. "We can do that anytime. Let's find a private spot, drink our wine, and see what happens. I'm really digging this whole scene. And if they get somebody else good to play, we don't want to miss that."

"Okay," I agree. It's time for Joel to head home... if it weren't for the faire, he would already have left. Any concert at my place would end up being a short one. We gather up our stuff and head to the next field. We wade through tall grass and wild oats and spread our blanket underneath a big eucalyptus tree. Any minute now, I expect to see police helicopters.

My hand slips into my pocket and I feel the smooth contours of the cat goddess. Protection. Having her in my pocket makes me feel safer.

We sit on the blanket and lean our backs against the tree trunk. Joel opens the wine and we pass it back and forth. It's sweet and I love the way it warms me all the way down from my throat to my belly. Music starts up, but from where we sit, we can't tell what band it is.

Joel hands me the bottle. He picks up a bell-shaped eucalyptus bud and sniffs it. "I'm thinking about writing a book," he says.

I turn and stare at him. "What about?" I ask. "These crazy times we're living in?"

He drops the bud and looks up at the dark blue evening sky. "Yeah that, and about work, the way people get trapped in these dead-end, meaningless jobs—that's where they want us. They sure don't want us getting any ideas about changing things for the better—no way. They want everybody to be mindless fodder for their wars and their corporate money machine."

"Wow!" I put my hand on his arm. "I can't wait to read it. I used to write stories."

"Really?" Joel turns toward me. "What kind of stuff did you write?"

"It was a long time ago..." Oh God—that's what I should be doing! What happened? Why did I stop? I take a big gulp of wine and pass the bottle to Joel. "I started a novel in high school about a girl who ran away and joined the beats," I say. "But now, every time I get an idea, there's always some shitty academic paper I have to write instead. With creativity, you've got to write it when the idea hits. You can't just plan to write it later because it dries up. Dies. Disappears. Don't let that happen to you!" I pick up a dead leaf and begin shredding it.

He slips his arm around my shoulders. "Yeah, I know what you mean," he says. "This fucking job I have—I sure like the money but I hate the job, the room I have to do it in, and most of all, the other people. You know how people talk about 'company men'—well, there really *are* company men. So I'll write a book about a fucked pincock in some government bureaucratic job and the daily humiliations he goes through for years until he either goes completely insane or kills himself, I haven't decided which."

It's a wonderful idea. "Oh, have him go insane," I say. I press my face against his neck, kiss the hollow under his jaw, then pull back and look him in the eye. "It could end up with him babbling all this stuff that doesn't make any sense on one level but on a deeper level it's totally right on. It could be kind of eerie and the reader wouldn't quite know how to interpret it."

He grins back at me, excited now. "Yeah, there could be this monologue at the end—it wouldn't be clear where it was coming from—whether he had killed himself or not—"

"Wait!" I break in. "It just occurred to me—the dude's not in prison. Why didn't he *quit* the job if he hated it that much?"

Joel chuckles. He pulls me up against him and puts his mouth to my ear. "Because not only is he a fucked pincock, he's a *weak* fucked pincock."

I lean against him. I lift the bottle out of his hand, tip it up to my mouth, and take another swallow of sweet wine. "So did he have a bunch of things happen during his childhood to make him that way?"

"Yeah, there'll be a bunch of flashbacks." Joel takes the bottle from me. "During his whole life, the son of a bitch *never* stood up for himself. It's like he's genetically defective or something."

"So for sure this isn't a hero's journey." I like his idea more and more.

"Hell no. For every hero's journey there are hundreds, maybe thousands of lives that are the complete opposite of a hero's journey. *That's* what I'm going to write about." He slams the bottle down for emphasis.

I put one leg across Joel's legs. His arms hold me close. I run my finger over the brass lion's head buckle on his belt. It looks like Aslan in the Narnia books. Faint music plays in the distance, but we don't recognize the songs. "I think your idea is fantastic," I say.

"School's almost over," Joel reminds me. "Then you can start writing your own stuff again. We'll both write—keep each other going."

A stream of cop cars comes down the road, lights flashing. Joel takes another swig and screws the cap on the bottle as police cars surround the Pleasure Faire. We get to our feet, fold up the blanket with the wine bottle inside, and ease farther away, keeping to the shadows. The music comes to an abrupt stop. A police bullhorn squawks. Because of the direction of the wind or the distance, we can't make out the words, but the people's angry shouting needs no interpretation.

"Shit," Joel says. "I better get out of here before they close off the roads."

People run and stumble across El Colegio like a herd of steers during a wild west cattle drive. The cops whoop behind them like crazed cowboys.

A few hundred yards away, Joel and I cross the road by ourselves and stroll down the dark streets. The Bug waits for us like an old friend. Joel puts the blanket on top of the car and digs in his pocket for his keys. I lean back against the hood. The metal is friendly. It welcomes my butt.

Joel unlocks the passenger door, opens it and tosses the blanket in the back seat. He holds the door open and sweeps his arm out sideways. I start to get in and he grabs my shoulder, pulls me up against him, and gives me a plum wine kiss. "Okay, get in." While he goes around to the driver's side, I slide into the passenger's seat and lean across the console to pop the lock for him. He gets in behind the steering wheel, slides the key into the ignition, and puts the car in gear. I lean back and inhale the salty smell of stale corn nuts. Sand crunches under my butt. The ordinariness is so comforting.

We don't encounter any police and in another moment, Joel pulls into the driveway of our duplex. We get out of the car and lean against each other as we go up the concrete steps.

In the living room, June sprawls on the sofa with a yellow marker and one of her class notebooks open on her lap. She's barefoot, in gray sweatpants and a red T-shirt. Taj Mahal is on the record player, singing the blues.

Joel goes in the bedroom.

"Did you go to the faire?" I ask June.

"Yeah. When Taj didn't show up, I left. I didn't see you guys."

"Bummer—you could've hung out with us." I sit down on the end of the couch and June moves her feet to make room.

She snaps her notebook shut and puts the cap on her yellow marker. "Did they end up with a decent band after all?"

"I don't know," I say. We split too, sat under a tree in a field and drank wine. We saw the pigs come squealing up; they shut the whole faire down."

"God, that's so fucked!" She swats the couch cushion with her notebook. "Why won't they leave us alone?"

I shake my head. "I don't know. You'd think they're deliberately trying to start a riot."

Joel comes out with his wetsuit and odds and ends of clothing. His surfboard leans against the living room wall and he hefts it along with the clothes.

I get to my feet. "Can I help with that?"

'Naw, I've got it." I follow him out to the bug. He opens the door, tosses the clothes on the passenger seat, and straps the surfboard onto the rack on the metal roof. At last he turns to face me. "Okay, Darlin'. I'd better get going."

I move in close, wrap my arms around him and he pulls me up tight against him. I nuzzle my chin into his shoulder. "Be careful," I say.

He kisses me and shoves his hands first into my back pockets, then under my jeans. He squeezes my bare butt. "Keep that warm for me," he growls.

"Always," I say.

He jumps into the car. The engine starts and we blow each other kisses. I stand in the driveway as he backs out and heads down Sabado Tarde. The red taillights get smaller and smaller until he turns a corner and they disappear. A familiar ache throbs in my chest. A chill sense of doom like a pestilence looms over this town. Every time he leaves, I feel like this time it will be forever.

Heavy with sadness, I hang onto the metal railing and drag myself up the steps. I'm glad for the warm lamplight inside and Taj on the record player.

"I know how you feel," June says. "Every time Will leaves... What the fuck are we doing here?"

"Living in a police state." I go over to the kitchen sink and get myself a glass of water.

"But they can't keep us here after finals. Just a couple more weeks and this will be over."

Oh God, she's right! What am I going to do? "You gonna move in with Will?" I say.

"Uh huh. I'm gonna miss this place like hell though—the way it *was*."

"Yeah…" My eyes sting and my throat is tight. "This was the *best* place in the world."

The phone rings and I rush back into the kitchen to pick it up. It's Joel.

"Hi Darlin'. I'm in Goleta—just wanted to let you know, there's about a thousand people down at the loop throwing rocks and fire bombs at the bank. People are really pissed off about the way they closed the faire down."

"Oh, shit. Here we go again," I groan.

"I know. I passed dump trucks coming in on my way out. Lock your door and all your windows."

"At least I know you got out safe." A surge of love warms my chest and trickles down into my belly. He stopped at a pay phone to let me know! "Thanks for calling. I love you so much."

"Love you too. Miss you already."

"Me too."

"Bye."

I set the receiver in its cradle and go back to the living room. June has opened her notebook again. Her legs are curled underneath her on the sofa cushion.

I wander over to the pillow corner but I'm too restless to sit down. I come back to the coffee table and stand next to it. I nudge the wooden leg with my toe. "There's another riot at the bank," I tell June. "Joel passed dump trucks coming in on his way out of IV."

June rolls her eyes. "And why am I not surprised?" She slams her notebook down on the coffee table, uncurls her legs, and gets to her feet. "I am so fuckin' sick of all this!"

And so it all begins. Again.

All through the night, the trucks rumble past our duplex and wake us up every time we drift off. Some time in the middle of the night, yelling right outside our apartment jerks me out of a nightmare about black-robed executioners with axes. I sit on the edge of my bed, flooded with terror. I creep out into the living room and meet June on her way to the window behind the sofa. We kneel on the couch and peek through the crack between the curtains. There's a patrol car right in our driveway! We drop the curtain, jump back and shove the sofa in front of the door.

We kneel on the floor and peek out again. The lights are on in the apartment across from ours. Two police officers drag John, our surfer neighbor, over to the car. He's a friend of Joel's and has a mane of blond hair like Joel used to have. His hands are behind his back, in handcuffs. Another cop drags John's girlfriend Lisa out by her long, red hair. They shove John and Lisa in the back of the patrol car and go back into the apartment. In a moment, they frog-march John's roommate Larry out of the apartment, holding his arms behind his back while they shove him forward. Larry stumbles and one of the cops smacks him on the side of the head with his club before they cram him into the car with John and Lisa. A cop goes back and turns the lights out, then the car backs out of the driveway.

June slides off her knees, back to the wall, legs stretched out on the carpet. "What the fuck was that about?"

"That was the Gestapo," I say, "or the KGB." When I was little, Daddy loved to hold forth at the dinner table about what happens when the Communists take over. The secret police come to your house in the middle of the night, take you away, and nobody ever knows what happened. You just disappear. His stories gave me nightmares and made me wet the bed.

June stares at me, eyes wide. She presses her fingers against her teeth. "Did you see Lisa? She was barefoot. In a skimpy little nightgown. Those bastards dragged her out of bed!"

I freeze. I pull my knees up to my chest and wrap my arms around them, make myself as small as I can. "Oh, my God. If a bunch of Nazis broke in and grabbed you while you were asleep—can you imagine?"

"I don't think I'd ever get over it." Tears fill her eyes and her face crumples. "Those guys were home the whole time. No way were they involved in any riot."

"So it must have been random. They were just looking for a place to break in. It could just as easily have been us." I curl myself into a tight little ball.

June stares at me. "What if they come back?"

I uncurl and jump to my feet. "We better get dressed!"

With a big sniff, she swipes her arm across her eyes and gets up. We rush into our rooms. I pull on the jeans I wore to the faire. I take the little statue of the goddess Bast from the dresser and slip it into my pocket. I open the top dresser drawer and pull out a pair of socks. I sit on the bed while I pull them on and slide my feet into my Redwing boots. I pull a sweatshirt over my head, thrust my arms into the sleeves and give the bottom of it a good yank. I pick up *The Complete Works of Shakespeare* and *The Norton Anthology of English Literature,* thick hardback books, and carry them out to the living room. I shove the books under the edge of the couch to wedge it so it won't slide easily if the police bash down the door.

June comes out in jeans and a plaid flannel shirt, Keds on her feet. "Great idea—those books," she says as I straighten up.

"What do we do if they break in?" I ask.

"It'll take them a while—at least we'll know they're coming. Let's barricade ourselves in my room and if we hear them at the front door, we can punch a hole in the screen and go out the window." She gives me a grim nod.

I nod back. "Good plan," I say.

In June's room, we lock the door and shove the back of her desk chair under the knob. We sit crosslegged on the bed, backs against the wall. "If they do get us," I say, "at least it won't be as much fun for them. They get off on jumping people who are sound asleep. They feed on panic. It really revs them up."

"From now on, we sleep in our clothes," June decides.

We sit in the dark. We strain our ears listening for tires in the driveway, stealthy footsteps outside, or whispers, but the only sound is the rumble of dump trucks making their sweeps through the neighborhood.

"Might as well see if we can get some rest," June says at last. "Looks like maybe they're going to skip us tonight… maybe… this is totally fucked, not being safe in our own apartment."

We lie side by side on the narrow bed. Death feels very close. It's an icy vapor, like that Dracula movie where the vampire can dissolve into mist and seep through the crack under the door. For the first time in years, I remember Claudia, a girl at my high school. She was everything I ever wanted to be—gorgeous red hair that fell to her waist while Mother forced haircuts and ugly, frizzy permanents on me every few months. Claudia's clothes were expensive and beautiful—black turtleneck sweaters and Moroccan embroidered vests, short black wool skirts, black tights, and Capezios on her tiny feet. She must have had every single style Capezio made! She was one of the few girls in the school who had her own car, a VW Bug like Joel's. High on pot one night, she and her boyfriend drove down the winding coast highway toward Big Sur. Nobody knew what happened, why they drove off a cliff and plunged hundreds of feet to the rocks below, but the next morning in P.E. class, one of the other girls told me Claudia was dead. She was sixteen.

The teachers and school staff never mentioned her death. School went on as though she had never existed, but I thought of nothing else for weeks. She was the first person I knew who was my age and had died. I hadn't known her well, had never been invited to her house, but she symbolized everything I longed to be, everything my parents wouldn't allow me to be, and now she was dead. I lay awake night after night. What was it like? Whatever death was, Claudia had experienced it. I could not believe that she was in hell. Either death was the end and we wink out forever, or...

Or what? I think now. What happens to us? I get up and gaze out the window. The sky is vast, endless, sprinkled with stars that have burned out long ago but are so far away that it has taken millions of years for their light to reach us. I feel like a tiny, meaningless speck in a gigantic, unfeeling universe full of dead stars and it scares the shit out of me.

The governor and the police have stepped up their attacks. It's their last chance to obliterate us before we graduate or leave for the summer. Will I survive long enough to graduate? I doubt that I will. What I know is that if I die, my parents will never question the atrocities that happened here. They'll blame me for provoking my own death. They'll say I deserved it. It won't even occur to them to try to get justice. There will be no help from them; I'm on my own.

13

MANNING THE BARRICADES

I never imagined I'd be a guerilla fighter. I didn't plan to be on my knees in the damp grass, head and shoulders under the house, feeling around among cobwebs and dirt for the rotten two by four I'd shoved into the crawl space this morning. June and I look for trash during the day and stash it under the duplex until night falls, when it's time to build the barricades to keep the police dump trucks out. I drag the board across the yard and up the street and add it to a stack of broken furniture, rugs, mattresses, and an old washing machine piled at the intersection. I swipe my sleeve across my sweaty forehead and roll my achy shoulders. Sabado Tarde is blocked. The street lights sizzle and spit in the fog. Smoke from fires mixed with tear gas drifting over from the next block stings my eyes and makes my nose run. The smoke and chemicals give the fog a faint yellowish tinge. I blink, squeeze my watery eyes shut, open them, and blink again. I poke a broken chair farther into the pile as a guy in a black sweatshirt pours a can of gasoline over the old junk. I back away and stand next to June. She holds out her hand and we slap our palms together. We don't know any of the other people here.

"Okay, everybody stand back!" The guy with the gas can tosses a match and flames erupt just as a police dump truck rounds the corner up ahead. We all run in different directions. I sprint up the street, cut between buildings, and dash into the courtyard of an apartment complex. I squeeze into the shrubbery in the shadows beyond the blue glow of the swimming pool. My heart slams in my chest and my fists clench so tight my nails dig into my palms. My breath comes in gasps. I got away this time. I can't panic now—there's more work to do. I focus on my breath, make it slow and deep. They can't see me here. They'll never find me...

It feels like I'm two different people; I study like crazy and write my final term papers during the day, then I go help man the barricades at night. I just can't go on hiding behind the couch pushed in front of our apartment door, waiting for the police to break in and drag me out by my hair. What value is a lifetime obeying orders, cringing and cowering while the police rampage through the streets? Where is the dignity in that? Staying inside doesn't make us safe—the police are completely out of control now. There are hundreds of them, called in from LA and Ventura and God knows what other towns to seize and destroy, kick doors down, and drag the people out. Larry and John and Lisa never came back. June and I peeked in their windows the morning after they were taken away and their apartment was ransacked, just trashed, cushions ripped off the couch and chairs, pieces of John's surfboard in the middle of the living room floor—how do you break a surfboard? Shards of broken dishes lay everywhere. Where are Larry and John and Lisa now? Maybe they're in jail with nobody to bail them out, the way I'll be when they haul me away, but more likely they're dead. The night they were dragged off was a turning point for June and me. We have to save our town. We go out in the street every night with people we've never met and put up barricades made out of old cars, pieces of lumber, discarded furniture, garbage cans, broken glass—anything we can find. When we take breaks from our studies during the day, we paint boards black and hammer nails in them so the points stick out the other side. At night we lay them in the street as invisible traps to puncture the tires of police vehicles. Sometimes the trucks turn around; sometimes they plow through. The minute they go around the corner, we come out of our hiding places in stairwells and behind buildings and in the shrubbery and get back to work piling up more junk to halt their progress next time around.

A helicopter circles overhead like a Nazgul's black dragon. I shiver in my army jacket and stay under cover until it passes. Sweat seeps into my socks. I'm wearing my heavy boots and if this doesn't build up my strength for climbing up mountains and rock jumping, I don't know what will. But it makes no difference now. I will either be "disappeared" or shot in the street. I hope I get shot—the thought of being disappeared turns my legs to Jell-o and I sink down until I'm sitting in the dirt. In earlier days, resisters carried cyanide capsules in case they got caught; they would kill themselves before they were tortured into giving away their comrades. In the existentialism class I took with Velvet, we read Andre Malraux's book *Man's Fate*, a novel about a failed communist revolution in China. The hero, Katow, gives his own cyanide to a couple of terrified youngsters while his comrades are being taken one by one to be thrown into a steam engine boiler and burned alive. Katow holds one of the boy's hands while he dies, and then it's his turn. As they drag him away, he tells himself, "Let's suppose I died in a fire."[1] God—could I ever be that brave?

Back on Sabado Tarde, somebody has put stereo speakers in an upstairs window. A Rolling Stones song blasts out into the street, "You Can't Always Get What You Want..."[2] I stand still, my boots riveted to the asphalt as the music washes over me. The long choral part at the end climbs up the scale. It builds and builds—gorgeous music like a heavenly choir of angels. It's a beautiful portrayal of death, the soul rising up from the body and drifting away free at the end. When I told June about this, we were on the couch with a carton of chocolate ice cream while the record played.

"Can't you just see it?" I said. "Doesn't it seem like death to you?"

June laughed. "No way!" she said with a grin. "That, my dear, is an orgasm."

I was in high school when the Rolling Stones burst into the middle of the British pop scene. I loved the Beatles, Hollies, and Gerry and the pacemakers. They were all so adorable in their identical suits and Beatle boots and bowl haircuts. All the girls I knew loved the bands, the music, and the new "mod" fashions. The Rolling Stones slammed onto that stage with throbbing guitars, wailing harmonicas, and Mick Jagger. What a voice he had. They were scruffy, bluesy, raw. I had such a crush on Keith Richards. Even then, he played the guitar like nobody else, and he looked like he wouldn't take shit from anybody.

The police in England hate the Stones the same way the Santa Barbara police hate students. They treated Isla Vista like a crime scene long before there were any riots or protests. Patrol cars have always been a constant presence on the loop, and undercover narcs lurked everywhere hoping for the chance to bust someone for a pitiful little stash. If their searches came up empty, the cops weren't above planting drugs in a suspect's pocket. The dealers they left alone. The Stones were hounded just like we were; twenty police raided Keith's house one afternoon. They arrested Mick for a measly four amphetamine pills and sentenced him to three months in jail—but Keith was sentenced to a year in Wormwood Scrubs Prison for pot. The whole idea was to make an example of Mick and Keith, but instead, it made them seem just like us. Now people all over the world see them as comrades. Their music is for times like these when the shit comes down—music that gives us the courage to do what needs to be done.

Somebody starts the record over and the driving opening guitar licks of "Gimme Shelter"[3] blast out into the street.

"Hey Kate!" somebody says behind me. My breath catches in my throat and I spin around, all nerves and adrenaline. It's David. He has traded his purple clothes for drab olive green from the Army surplus store. I'm so glad to see someone I know that I throw my arms around him.

He hugs me back. "Wow! Look at you! Street fighting woman—cool shit-kicking boots you've got there."

"Thanks." I grin. I picture him as a guerrilla fighter in the Bolivian jungle where Che made his last stand. He has painted black zigzags on his cheeks and has pulled his long red-gold hair back into a ponytail. "What're you doing all the way down Sabado Tarde?" I ask. David lives way on the other side of the loop, right across the street from Cyril and Velvet.

"I'm making my way around the barricades—Look what I scored!" He holds up a spool of metal wire. "Been stringing this across every street I can—knock down those son of a bitches in the truck beds."

My eyes practically bug out of their sockets when I see that wire. Yes! "Far out!" I say. "Maybe this'll finally stop them."

"Let's do it!" He unwinds some wire and hands it to me. I loop the end of the wire around a telephone pole and twist it tight while David runs across the street and secures the other end to a tree. Wire cutters come out of his pocket and we're done. I help him put another wire across farther down the street toward the loop. That ought to topple the cops standing in the truck beds. We move up to Trigo Road and string more wire until the spool is empty.

The deep rumble of a truck engine warns us that they're coming back. The huge tires make the asphalt vibrate. David throws his empty spool on a burning barricade and we dash behind a building and duck down under a stairwell. Somebody's already here—a blonde chick wearing a navy blue Sigma Chi sweatshirt that hangs down below her butt. She's got a big rock in her hand. I can't believe it. I stay cool and try not to stare; I never expected sorority debutantes to be out on the streets. My first year in the dorm, one of the girls, Barb, was rushing, trying to get into one of the sororities. I couldn't imagine going to rush parties and having all these girls looking me over and deciding whether I was good enough to be in their sorority, and I asked Barb, "Why would you put yourself through that?" "If you get in," she told me, "there are incredible social advantages." But Barb didn't make it in. I don't know if this girl's in a sorority, but I admire the fuck out of her. She's got a boyfriend in Sigma Chi so she's probably a Kappa or a Delta Phi Epsilon or... She's way out of her element, whatever she is.

"Cops been hassling you?" I ask.

She looks us over, lips pressed tight, eyebrows bunched together as she checks us out. Then her forehead smoothes and her mouth relaxes. "They shot tear gas right into our house!" Outrage quivers in her voice. "We've got this elderly lady in the house, she's like our housemother, about 90, and she was having trouble breathing, getting really sick. They've got the town closed off—what if we need to get her to the hospital? She could die!"

"Yeah, she could," I say. "This is so awful." I don't say "fucked;" I don't want to alienate the chick.

She flips her hair back. "So I decided to come out here and join you guys. I'll probably get kicked out of the sorority if they find out, but what's happening is so totally wrong!"

The dump truck rolls by and she rushes out, heaves her rock at it, and ducks behind a bush.

David and I stare at each other. "Now I've seen everything," he says.

"All my stereotypes just got blasted to smithereens," I agree.

Stringing wire across the street seemed like such a great idea, but somehow it doesn't work; the huge vehicles just blast through like tanks, and in a moment, they're gone.

David slumps, sits down on the stairs we were hiding behind, and puts his face in his hands. I sit beside him, slip my arm around him and lean my head against his shoulder. "I don't know how they got through, but at least we tried."

"I thought we'd stop them for sure," he says.

"Come on—we've got to keep fighting." I grab his hand, give it a tug. "Let's go. We can't give up!"

David gets to his feet. I look around for the sorority chick. I want to bring her with us, to protect her, keep her under my wing, but I don't see her anywhere. She's moved on.

We go back to my duplex on Sabado Tarde and drag a broken chair out from under the building. David takes it to the burning barricade and throws it in. I'm right behind him with a big chunk of driftwood. Everything feels like it's happening in slow motion, the way time stands still before you die. We make the fire burn as bright as we can before they come with their heavy artillery and gun us down. We'll stay until the very end.

It's the tenth of June. The school year is almost over. I sit on the grass with Velvet and Cyril and a thousand other people gathered in Perfect Park to defy the curfew. A lot of the university professors have come to show their support. I get a big lump in my throat and tears in my eyes, just as I did when I saw the middle-aged "straight" people at the march in San Francisco the day I met Joel. There's Dr. Spender, the silver-haired Shakespeare professor. After the way the University made an example of Bill Allen because of his views, I'm amazed to see him here even as the helicopters circle overhead, just as I can't believe I'm alive. I don't know how I've escaped being killed or dragged off to jail, but none of the people manning the barricades have been caught. Maybe the police are afraid of us. Instead of going after us, they raid apartments and kick down doors, handcuffing and beating people entirely at random the way they did with John, Larry, and Lisa.

Velvet is all in black, mourning our town. I gaze at her black pants and sweater and wish I had thought to wear black too, instead of my usual blue jeans. Velvet is always right-on. She cranes her head around, searching. "Where's June?"

"She's down in LA with Will," I say. "Lovin' Spoonful concert."

Her eyes get wide. "You mean you're all alone?"

"Yep." I make my voice nonchalant. I swipe my hand across the front of my white T-shirt and wipe off an imaginary bit of dirt. "She'll be back tomorrow."

Cyril is up on his knees with his camera. The shutter clicks as he snaps photos in all directions. He turns the camera on me and snaps a picture. "What are your plans for the summer?" he asks.

"Joel wants me to move in with him," I say. "Are you guys staying in Isla Vista?" I shade my eyes with my hand and peer up at the circling choppers.

"Yeah, I've still got more classes at Brooks." He sits back down.

"I'm going to try and get a job while he finishes," Velvet tells me. "No real jobs in Santa Barbara, but I could probably type things, something like that."

A helicopter hovers overhead. "This is an unlawful assembly!" a thunderous voice blasts out of a bullhorn above us. "You are ordered to disperse immediately or be arrested for curfew violation!" Fear constricts my chest like an icy fist, making my breathing shallow and rapid even before the tear gas that we all know will come. If only Joel were here, holding my hand! What am I going to do if we get arrested? Call my parents? No, I'll have to call Joel. Sound trucks and the helicopter all blast out orders for us to leave. Someone starts singing and we all join in. "Oh beautiful for spacious skies…" We go on to *The Star Spangled Banner* as patrol cars roll in and surround the park like the dark riders of Mordor. Hordes of police pour out and form columns like an army of orcs. We all chant "The Whole World is Watching" as cops drag people away from the edges of the demonstration. The arrests go on and on until darkness falls and the police draw closer to the middle of the crowd where we sit. Everyone links arms.

A gas fogger truck rolls up. Choking clouds of tear gas billow over us. We lie face-down on the grass, our arms over our heads but the gas seeps in anyway. I can't stop coughing; by this time, everybody I know in Isla Vista has respiratory problems. All I can think of is getting home to make some fenugreek tea. I'll make it especially strong this time. The brew is yellow like pee and doesn't taste much better, but of all the home remedies, it works best for opening congested, irritated airways. Police wade into the crowd with clubs and Velvet, Cyril, and I crawl away on our hands and knees toward the edge of the demonstration and away from the park. The cops aren't arresting anyone now; they're just clubbing people while more and more tear gas fills the air. I get separated from Velvet and Cyril. I get to my feet and thread my way through the crowd until I'm on Trigo. I cough so hard I throw up in the Rexall parking lot. I wipe my mouth on my T-shirt sleeve and stumble down the dark street.

"Hey Kate!" someone behind me calls.

I'm so weary I almost don't answer. How much longer can I go on? But I make myself stop and look around. A surfer dude walks up fast. My mouth drops open. "John!"

"Mind if we walk home together?"

"Oh God, John—June and I saw the pigs drag you out that night! I really thought you were dead..." I cough some more.

John pounds me on the back. "You okay?"

"Yeah," I gasp. "Really bad tear gas." I wipe away strings of saliva with the back of my hand. "What happened to you?"

A loud sigh bursts out of him. "I don't even want to talk about what their jail was like, way overcrowded, people crammed so tight in the cells we couldn't lie down... I finally got let go with no charges, but I don't know if I'll ever be able to use my hands again. They had me in these tight plastic handcuffs that cut off the circulation."

We get to my apartment. "Come on in," I say. "You don't even want to look at what they did to your place until morning." I unlock the door and switch on the light. I go straight to the kitchen, fill the kettle from the sink faucet and put it on the stove. John follows me and sits on one of the kitchen chairs. I splash water in my face, bathe my eyes, and use the dishtowel to dry off. I get the teapot and the green and white box of Seelect fenugreek seeds out of the cupboard. While I wait for the water to boil, I sit down at the table. John's face is haggard, eyes sunken but he gives me a rueful smile. His mop of blond hair is tangled and he has several days' growth of stubble.

"How's Joel? You know, I'm thinkin' he was really smart to flunk out of school before all this shit came down."

"He's fine. Actually, he comes back here every weekend. His car got hit by a bullet." I want to get a look at John's hands but they're on his lap, under the table.

"Yeah, I know. I went surfing with him a couple of times. You know how we were raised, all the talk about how America means freedom, democracy, the whole bit? I guess getting shot at made Joel realize how things really are, but for me it never sank in until they were dragging me out in the middle of the night. God—they were like fuckin' orcs out of *The Lord of the Rings*!"

"I know." I fold my hands on the table, then I wring my fingers and twist them. I pick up the salt shaker and set it down again. "John, ever since that night, June and I and a lot of other people have been out on the streets, building barricades, trying to save this place."

His breath whooshes out and he gives me a worried frown. "Lisa and Larry must be around *somewhere*. Have you heard from them?"

"No. I thought you guys were dead. But since they eventually let *you* go… I'll bet they're okay. Their parents probably bailed them out." I hope I'm right. The teakettle starts to whistle and I get up. I spoon some yellow fenugreek seeds into the teapot and pour boiling water over them. I lean over the kettle and breathe some of the steam. "I'm making fenugreek—for bad lungs. Want some?"

"Sure."

I pour two mugs of the yellow brew and bring them to the table. John wraps his hands around his cup; they are mottled and purplish. Fenugreek tastes pretty awful, but it soothes my throat and by the time I've drunk the first mug, I can breathe better.

"Were you at the demonstration in the park tonight?" I say.

"Yeah, for a while." His hands shake as he sets his cup down. "But when the pigs started dragging people away, I freaked and ran— if they arrest me again, no way will I get off without any charges! I was outta there before they started gassing everybody."

I push my chair back, grab the phone off the counter, and set it on the table next to him. "Why don't you call Lisa's parents? I'll bet that's where she is."

He reaches into his back pocket and fumbles for a moment. He stands up. "Can you get my wallet out? My fingers don't work anymore."

I pull the wallet out and put it in his hand. He's got a card with his phone numbers in there, and while he's making the call, I get a couple of spare blankets out of my bedroom closet and make a bed for him on the couch. I go back to the kitchen and pour myself another cup of tea.

John hangs up the phone. "You were right," he says. "Lisa's folks bailed her out and she's down in LA with them. Larry was in the hospital with a head injury, but he's okay now too."

There is no final exam for my 20th Century Literature class; we're here to pick up our final term papers with their grades. I take my seat in the front row as other people file in. Randy Greene, in khakis and workboots, clomps over to his seat by the window and slides into the chair. "Don't know why I came," he says. "I know he'll have just reamed me out—if I get a C-minus I'll be lucky."

"Yeah," someone says.

"No shit," says the guy next to me, and all over the room, we murmur agreement.

Professor Frazier strides in wearing a herringbone tweed jacket, lugging a fat black briefcase. He sets the briefcase down and stands in front of the desk. He gazes at us for a long moment. His sandy, gray-streaked hair has grown shaggy and covers the tops of his ears, and his grizzly beard is trimmed to about half an inch. A rush of regret swells up in my throat. Dr. Frazier's class was wonderful and I wish I had written a paper to do him proud.

"What a year this has been." He sighs. "They arrested me at Perfect Park; I've just come from jail. But I have news. Today, Judge Lodge dismissed the charges and released over 300 people who were arrested at the park Wednesday night. The curfew is lifted to 11 p.m., and the LA goon squad has been sent back to whatever section of hades they came from."

We all stand up and cheer. We clap and clap.

Professor Frazier crosses his arms, leans back on the desk, and smiles. Never have I loved him more.

"The demonstration did some good after all," he says as the applause dies down. He goes around to the front of the desk, opens the briefcase, and takes out a big stack of papers. "It has been a real pleasure having all of you in class, and a privilege to read the wonderful papers that you somehow managed to write in the midst of apocalypse. You're heroes—I have given you all A's."

In the corridor after class, I feel like I'm floating above the pavement as I walk to the bike racks. I got an A! And all those people they dragged out of the park are free! I dig the key to my bike lock out of my pocket… No bicycle! Huh? I search up and down the rack. Maybe I forgot where I left it? But it's gone, stolen. I cram the key back in my pocket and start down the path toward home. It doesn't matter. I don't need a bike anymore. The sun warms my back and I can smell the ocean. I feel sort of glad—My butt won't have to endure that horrid plastic seat ever again!

The Doors play while June and I sort through our things, putting stuff in boxes. On the coffee table is a half-gallon economy-size bottle of Gallo vin rose, along with a package of fat crinkle-cut potato chips and a bag of Pepperidge Farm Milano cookies.

The pillow corner belongs to June and she crams the purple cushions into a big plastic bag. That corner felt like home and it looks so lonely and bare now. I pour more wine into my glass and take a big gulp to keep from crying. I wish I had taken a picture of that pillow corner, but I don't own a camera.

June's last final is over. Mine, in art history, is two days from now. June lugs another box out of her bedroom and sets it next to her stack of belongings in the middle of the living room floor. She goes into the kitchen and I hear the clatter of silverware.

I fill a box with books from the brick-and-board bookshelf, then straighten up. I wipe my dusty hands on my jeans and pad barefoot into the kitchen. June crouches in front of one of the floor-level cupboards. She pulls out a couple of enamel pans. She swipes her arm across her sweaty forehead and looks up at me. "Owning stuff really is a pain in the ass, you know?"

"Can I help?" I ask.

"Yeah—would you get me another glass of wine?"

I get a fresh glass out of the cupboard above the sink. "Comin' right up."

We pack June's dishes in sheets of newspaper. By the time we're done, we're both tipsy. June has newsprint smears on her khaki pants.

We go back to the living room, collapse on the sofa, and cram potato chips into our mouths.

"This is so weird to be leaving," June says. "After months of living in a police state." She picks up the bag of cookies and reaches inside.

"Fuck yes." I pick up my glass and take a huge swig. "Seems like just last night we were barricading the streets, running for our lives…"

"And now all of a sudden we're not students anymore. What the fuck do we do now? Will we turn into normal people?" She plonks her dirty bare feet on the coffee table and stares at me.

I stare back. "Wow. That's really heavy. I still get to be a student for a couple more days, but…"

"And then Joel'll come get you." She pulls a cookie out of the bag, bites off a third of it, and chews. "Will's coming to get me." She swallows and sets the bag back on the table. "Shit, Kate—do you *want* to live a normal life after all this?"

"Hell, no!" I wash my potato chip down with more wine.

"Me neither. I'm gonna go live with Will 'cuz I love the dude, but all the career plans I had feel like total bullshit to me after all that's happened."

"Yeah." I set my glass on the table. "Should we save the rest of the wine for Will?"

"No way!" June grabs the bottle. "If he wants some he can get it himself." She pours more wine into our glasses.

"I'm still basically the same person, I guess," I say. I sip my wine while I think it out. "You know—civil rights, protesting the war, and all—but now I realize how naïve I was. Now I don't think I'll ever fit into normal society. I really expected to die out there on the streets."

"Me too." June has tears in her eyes. "You know, I believe we *did* save this town. But not for ourselves. We saved it for the people to come."

14

LETTING IT BE

My final exams are over. No more last-minute cram sessions. No more slogging through my class notes and textbooks for the last time, trying to remember bits of information that I'll forget immediately after the exam. I've graduated. It doesn't seem real.

After the riots and the months of police occupation, Isla Vista has gone back to a weird semblance of normal. Being under siege seemed to go on forever. It felt like we were frozen in time, repeating the same moment over and over. Now I don't have to sneak around when I go outside at night. That doesn't feel real, either. I keep looking for police cars, but they don't patrol the neighborhoods now.

School is finished, but I just can't fit graduation into the person I am now after the things that happened. There's no place for it. It doesn't even occur to me to reserve a cap and gown. To wear something that reminds me of a 19th Century man's silk bathrobe and that ridiculous hat with the flat board on top—I did that before, when I graduated from high school, because my parents didn't allow me a choice. I have a choice now, and I skip my graduation ceremony. What in the world does that have to do with what happened here?

Everyone is leaving for the summer. Lost and shell-shocked, I wander up and down the empty streets. Charred bits of wood and pieces of broken furniture litter the intersections. The asphalt wavers in a limbo-like, in-between state. Everything looks bleached-out, like an overexposed photograph. The air shimmers, as if this place is about to wink out of existence forever.

The apartment is bare and empty without June's belongings, and my own half-filled boxes clutter the living room. It doesn't feel like home anymore. I pack up my things in a daze, and the more I pack, the lonelier I feel.

My parents expect me to return home and live with them after university. Mother says she can get me a job in the same office where she works, but after their not believing me when I told them about the riots, I can't imagine going back. And where does Joel fit into Mother's plan—or my own plans? I've been racking my brains, freaking out about what to do. It would be a lot easier to hit the road by myself if I had a car or at least someone to hitchhike with. I could do it alone, stick out my thumb and see what happens, but that's so scary and lonely. I don't know anyone. Jack Kerouac knew people in the towns he visited. He had some anchors along the coast. I'll be a complete stranger everywhere I go north of Southern California. Joel is the only anchor I have, and he doesn't want me to leave.

All last weekend, he begged me to come live with him and his parents for a while.

"Your *parents?*" I said. We were at the kitchen table with cups of tea from my Japanese teapot and bagels with cream cheese he had brought from home. I thought he must be joking, but he had that direct, thoughtful gaze that meant he was serious. "No!" I set my bagel down on my plate. "No way do I want to go live with your parents!"

"But we'll be together again, every day, not just once a week… we can figure the rest out later. We'll get a place of our own, and we can help each other with our writing. The most important thing is for us to be together."

He didn't have to say "together" very many times to wear me down.

Right now, I miss him so much I have to agree, being together *is* the most important thing.

I wander into the head shop. It smells so good inside, a wonderful combination of incense, fragrant wood, frankincense, patchouli and marijuana. Everywhere there are carved wooden boxes from India, silk scarves, woven shawls, and psychedelic posters. On the counter is a stack of Zap Comix, and in the glass case underneath are hookahs, hash pipes and roach clips hammered out by hand from brass wire. The rug is strewn with cushions to sit on. I choose one of the wooden boxes and take it up to the counter to buy.

The man behind the cash register has long light-brown hair and a scraggly beard. His eyes are bloodshot and red. He peers at the box. He opens the lid and looks inside. Nothing there. He picks it up, stares at it more closely, and sets it down. His bleary eyes swim around, then focus on me.

"Yes?" His voice is hoarse.

"I'd like to buy this box," I say.

"Oh." He pokes the box with his finger and it turns sideways. "I guess that would be cool."

The carpet feels soft under my bare feet. Music plays in the background. It's rock, but with sitars and tablas. You could trip out or even meditate to that melody.

"I love this music," I say. "What is it?"

"Saddhu Brand," the man says. He takes my five-dollar bill and hands me the box without giving me change. If I were that stoned, I couldn't make change either.

"I've never heard of that band," I say.

His red eyes lock on mine in an intense stare. "Nevertheless, it is Saddhu Brand."

I sit down on a velvet cushion and space out, lose myself in the music. It is so peaceful here; I could listen forever. Someone taps my arm and I look up. It's a little blond boy, about four, in a blue T-shirt and shorts. He holds out a toy house made of thin cardboard.

"Wow," I say. "That's really nice." I've seen these houses before; they come in a book and you punch them out and fold them and insert the tabs into slots to make houses.

"Want to play with me?" Now he looks sideways, not meeting my eyes. His bare feet go pigeon-toed and the toes wiggle.

"Sure," I say.

He looks right at me and grins. "I'll get the rest." He goes behind the counter and brings a paper bag. He turns it upside down and out fall more houses.

My new friend goes into the back of the store and comes back with a box of toy cars. He sits down on his heels, knees bent, and places the box between us. Where was he all this time? Sleeping back there?

"What's your name?" I ask.

"Dylan," he says.

We make a miniature town. We line the houses up along the concentric rectangles that make the border of the Persian carpet. The road between the houses is deep red. Dylan fills it with small metal cars with rubber wheels. He holds up a green Corvette. "My favorite car," he chortles.

I pick out a red Thunderbird with round porthole windows in the back. "I like this one," I say. I push it down the road. "Beep Beep!"

We both laugh.

The store proprietor slumps over the counter and dozes, head on his folded arms. The sitar twangs.

I watch Dylan push his car along between the houses. What a beautiful child—I'd love to be his mother. That's when it hits me. I've tried so hard to be a responsible adult that I've lost something precious. I can't even play with a kid without thinking about being his mother. I need to start over—learn to play like a child again. I don't want to lose that. All the other stuff can wait until I get done grooving on these little cardboard houses.

Dylan points to the biggest house. "This is where I live," he tells me.

The store owner wakes up and rubs his eyes. "OK, Dylan. Pick up your stuff—it's way past time to go home."

Dylan sticks out his lower lip. "No. I'm havin' fun."

"Pick it up, Dylan. Mom's waiting."

"I'll help you," I say. I set the cars' box on its side and drive the Thunderbird in. "Vroom, vroom!"

The dad comes around the counter. He stomps on the rug, and the houses sway and topple over. "Uh-oh—" he yells. "It's an earthquake!"

Dylan grins, and we make a game of putting the cars and houses away.

"Thanks for entertaining the kid," the dad says.

"I was the one being entertained. I totally grooved on being little again for a while. Thanks for playin' with me, Dylan."

"You're welcome." His smile makes me want to smother him with kisses. We all leave the shop. Dylan and his dad go toward a battered, rusty VW bus parked next to the curb. I head the other direction, toward home.

What I love most about this beach is the warm ocean water. In Northern California where I grew up, the water was so cold it made your feet ache and you had to put up with a good ten minutes of agony before they went numb. Here, though, the ocean is like a womb. It's like salty amniotic fluid. My feet sink into the wet sand with every step as the waves lap over them and splash my legs almost all the way up to my cutoff jeans. The water is cerulean blue, reflecting the sunlight in little sparkles. In the distance, near the horizon, I can just make out one of the channel islands.

A couple come skipping hand in hand down the wooden steps that zigzag to the top of the cliff. A big golden retriever runs ahead of them. Holding hands, they sit down on a log that washed up on the beach during a winter storm. As I pass by, the girl fondles her lover's curly black hair and they kiss. I keep walking. It feels good to breathe the salty air. I suck it deep into my tear-gassed lungs.

The dog races across the beach and plunges into the water in giant leaps.

"Outta sight!" I laugh. I jump up and down and lift my arms toward the sky.

He gallops up to me on the next wave, and we dash down the beach. He barks.

"Yeah! Yeah!" I yell. We leap and dance, run in a circle, into the water, then away again. The dog seems to laugh, tongue lolling out, eyes alight with mischief. What I love most about dogs is their joy. They don't try to be cool; they leap high in the air, spin in circles, and act goofy. I spin around too, like a crazy dog. We race far down the beach until I'm out of breath and can't run anymore. I turn around and head back the way we came to make sure my new friend gets back to his people. The couple he came with still sit on the log, kissing, a half-empty bottle of wine in the sand between them. They look up.

"Hey, thanks for playing with my dog," the guy says. "Not very many people would do that."

"I should thank *you*," I laugh. "What a great dog! What's his name?"

"Elrond." Hearing his name, the dog whips around and looks up at him. His golden plume tail sweeps from side to side.

I bend down, stroke the soft fur on top of his head, and kiss his wet black nose. "It was wonderful to meet you," I say.

He licks my face with his big, slobbery, pink tongue.

"Elrond!" scolds the girl.

"It's okay!" I laugh, and head up the stairs.

It's the last day of my lease. I sit on the front lawn surrounded by cardboard boxes crammed with all my belongings. I'm homesick already. I look back over my shoulder at the familiar, now empty apartment and tears well up. I swipe my arm across my eyes to keep them from spilling over. I dig my toes into the warm grass. Palm trees across the street sound like rain whenever a gust of ocean wind rustles their leaves. After fighting so hard to keep our town safe, leaving feels wrong. But I've graduated. I'm finished here; it's time to go.

Joel's Bug races up the street and screeches to a stop in front of the duplex. He leaps out and runs across the grass. A huge grin lights up his face. He's early. My sadness evaporates, and I grin back. I jump to my feet and step toward him and we come together in a wild embrace. He swings me in a big, glad circle and then I press myself tight against him. No sand and salt today; he smells like soap and fresh shampoo.

"Oh, *God*—I'm so glad you're here!" I sink my face into his white T-shirt.

"Me too—you can't even imagine how glad I am right now! Let's get your stuff loaded."

He was right. Being together *is* what matters; it's way more important than *where* we are. All the same, an ache rises in my chest and my throat tightens up as we load my boxes into the back seat of the Bug. I shove another carton in, turn around, and lean against the warm metal behind the car door.

"Wow, Joel," I say. "I can't believe I don't live here anymore. What was it like for you when you left IV? Was it hard?"

He lugs a heavy box full of books to the car. Back muscles straining, he crams it in. "Fuck yes!" The words come out in a gasp. "All this time, I've just existed between weekends when I could come back."

"I know," I say, and step away from the car. "Being separated was so hard."

He gives me the sweetest smile. "But we're together now."

The back seat is full. He opens the driver's door and pops the trunk. I lug my brown backpack and orange sleeping bag over and lay them on top of a car jack and some towels. "Oh, Joel—that meant so much to me that you still came back after it all turned into a war zone."

There's a clatter as he stuffs in a box of pans and kitchen utensils. "I shoulda been here the whole time. I *had* to come back. I screwed up, but this was our home—I couldn't let them take it away." He goes back for the last box, stuffs it in, and slams the trunk shut.

"I'm really going to miss it," I say.

"Yeah, me too. Leaving really sucked. At least we get to be together, but it'll be fuckin' weird, not making that drive back every weekend... have we got everything?"

I step onto the grass one last time. Nothing is left. "Goodbye," I whisper. Quick steps take me back to the car and I get in. Joel is already in the driver's seat.

He gives me an inquiring glance, eyebrows raised, one corner of his mouth lifted. "Ready?"

"Yeah." I stretch out my legs. The floorboards under my feet are gritty with sand.

Joel puts the key in the ignition and starts the engine.

The Beatles' "Let it Be"[1] plays on the car radio as we leave Isla Vista for the last time. I roll down my window and gaze at everything we pass. I try to turn my eyes into a camera lens, to store the Magic Lantern Theatre, Red Lion Books, Borsodi's coffee house, the Sun and Earth health food store, and of course the charred ruins of the bank forever in my memory. My throat swells and gets so scratchy I can't swallow. My last look at Isla Vista is through a haze of tears.

FOOTNOTES

CHAPTER 1

1. Hair: The American Tribal Love-Rock Musical, *Aquarius,* James Rado and Gerome Ragni, 1967

2. Phil Ochs, *I Ain't Marching Anymore,* 1965, Elektra Records

CHAPTER 4

1. Linda Ronstadt, *Long, Long Time,* Gary White, 1970, Capitol Records

CHAPTER 5

1. KCSB Audio Tapes, February 25, 1970, Kunstler Speech

2. The Band, *Up On Cripple Creek,* 1969, Capitol Records

CHAPTER 6

1. The Beatles, *Helter Skelter,* 1968, Apple Records

2. William Butler Yeats, *The Second Coming, Selected Poems and Two Plays of William Butler Yeats,* Collier Books, 1962

CHAPTER 7

1. Jefferson Airplane, *Lather,* 1968, RCA Records

2. Eric Burdon and the Animals, *When I Was Young,* 1967, MGM Records

CHAPTER 8

1. Bob Dylan, *Blonde on Blonde,* 1966, Columbia Records

CHAPTER 9

1. Bob Borsodi, handwritten sign

2. The Beatles, *Hey Jude,* 1968, Apple Records

3. KCSB, April 18, 1970, Shutdown, Cy Godfrey speaking

CHAPTER 10

1. Geoffrey Chaucer, *Selections from the Tales of Canterbury, and Short Poems,* Houghton Mifflin, 1966

2. Geoffrey Chaucer, *Selections from the Tales of Canterbury, and Short Poems,* Houghton Mifflin, 1966

3. The Doors, *The End,* 1967, Elektra Records

CHAPTER 11

1. Children of God, folded paper handout

2. Jeremiah 6:26

3. Children of God, folded paper handout

CHAPTER 13

1. Andre Malraux, *Man's Fate,* Translated by Haakon Chevalier, H. Smith and R. Haas, 1934

2. The Rolling Stones, *You Can't Always Get What You Want,* 1969, Decca

3. The Rolling Stones, *Gimme Shelter,* 1969, Decc

CHAPTER 14

1. The Beatles, *Let It Be,* 1970, Apple Records

ABOUT THE AUTHOR

Kate Comings received a B.A. in English from University of California, Santa Barbara. She has been a single mom and is a retired medical transcriptionist. An enthusiastic amateur photographer, she writes almost every day and and is working on a series of novels set in Portland, Oregon. She lives in Northeast Portland, Oregon with two dogs.

Made in the USA
Las Vegas, NV
26 November 2022